so simple
CROCHET

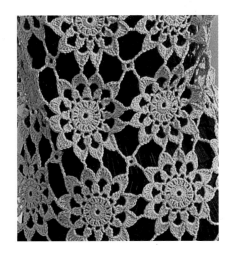

so simple
CROCHET

A fabulous collection of
24 fashionable and fun designs

Melody Griffiths

CRE▲TIVE
HOMEOWNER®

First published in North America in 2006 by

CREATIVE
HOMEOWNER®

Upper Saddle River, NJ
Creative Homeowner® is a registered trademark of
Federal Marketing Corporation

34103415 7/06

Current printing (last digit) 10 9 8 7 6 5 4 3 2 1
Library of Congress card number: 2005926423
ISBN 1-58011-276-5

Senior Editor: Clare Sayer
Production: Hazel Kirkman
Design: Isobel Gillan
Photographer: Sian Irvine
Editorial Direction: Rosemary Wilkinson

Reproduction by Pica Digital PTE Ltd
Printed and bound in Malaysia by Times Offset

CREATIVE HOMEOWNER
A division of Federal Marketing Corp.
24 Park Way
Upper Saddle River, NJ 07458
www.creativehomeowner.com

CONTENTS

INTRODUCTION

Couture crochet, easy crochet, fun accessories, or funky garments – everywhere you look fashion incorporates the look of traditional needlecraft. You too can create uniquely styled garments using this collection of 24 up-to-the-minute styles. Each piece is designed so that it is easy to make and wonderful to wear.

Crochet is one of the most rewarding and creative of the traditional needlearts. The stitches are easy to learn and the materials are easy to find. All you need is a crochet hook and some yarn but the patterned effects can vary enormously, from a lightweight lacy look to a densely textured surface.

In fact, all crochet stitches are based on the simple action of making loops with a hook, and once you've learned the basics, you'll find it surprisingly easy to master the different combinations of stitches and to create exciting, one-of-a-kind fashions.

Crochet is a two-handed process where the left hand controls the tension and gauge of the yarn as well as holds the work, while the right hand manipulates the hook. Most left-handed people find that they are comfortable working this way but if preferred, left-handers could reinterpret the directions included in the text, reading left for right and right for left, using a mirror, if necessary, to check the illustrations.

BASIC INFORMATION

Equipment

Crochet is an incredibly versatile craft – you can achieve the most wonderful effects with the simplest of materials. All you really need is a crochet hook but you may find some other sewing essentials useful.

CROCHET HOOKS

The one essential piece of equipment you need to crochet is a crochet hook. The smallest size hooks are generally made of steel and come in sizes 14 to 00.

They are mostly used for delicate lace work using very fine yarns. Medium size hooks between 2 and 10 are usually made of coated aluminum or, in sizes 2 to 8, bamboo. Large hooks in sizes 10 to Q are made of plastic and may be hollow to reduce the weight. Old hooks may be bone, ivory or Bakelite. Even if only one hook size is given in the instructions to make a garment, it's a good idea to buy the size above and the size below as well because you may need to change the hook size to obtain the correct gauge (see page 10).

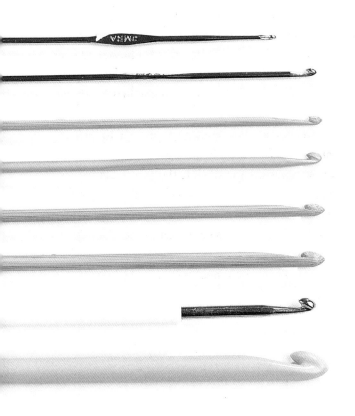

CROCHET HOOK CONVERSION CHART
Approximate sizes

US	Metric
B/1	2.25 mm
C/2	2.75 mm
D/3	3.25 mm
E/4	3.50 mm
F/5	3.75 mm
G/6	4.00 mm
7	4.50 mm
H/8	5.00 mm
I/9	5.50 mm
J/10	6.00 mm
K/10½	6.50 mm
L/11	8.00 mm
M/13	9.00 mm
N/15	10.00 mm
P/16	12.00 mm

OTHER EQUIPMENT

As well as a range of hooks, other items you'll need to make garments are a tape measure, markers, pins, a blunt-pointed sewing needle or a tapestry needle, and scissors.

Yarns

The projects in this book use a wide range of yarns. Classic crochet uses smooth yarn and this is probably the best choice for a beginner as it is easier to see the stitches. But, interesting effects can be obtained with the simplest of stitches and unusual, textured fashion yarns. Each project has been designed specifically for the yarn given in the instructions. This is not to say that the designs cannot be made using an alternative. However, yarns vary so much that the you may not get the correct gauge, the amount of yarn you need to buy could be different and the fabric you make may not behave in the same way as the original. Your choice could be a triumph or it could be a disaster, so if you do use a different yarn, be prepared for a different result. The fibre content and approximate yardages of the yarns used in this book are listed below.

Coats Anchor Arista: 80% viscose, 20 polyester. 110 yd/100 m per 1 oz (25 g) ball.

Debbie Bliss Cashmerino Aran: 55% merino, 33% microfibre, 12% cashmere. 98 yd/90 m per 1¾ oz (50 g) ball.

Debbie Bliss Cathay: 50% cotton, 35% microfibre, 15% silk. 110 yd/100 m per 1¾ oz (50 g) ball.

Debbie Bliss Cotton Angora: 80% cotton, 20% angora. 98 yd/90 m per 1¾ oz (50 g) ball.

Debbie Bliss Cotton Cashmere: 85% cotton, 15% cashmere. 104 yd/95 m per 1¾ oz (50 g) ball.

Debbie Bliss Maya: 100% wool slub. 137 yd/126 m per 3½ oz (100 g) ball.

Debbie Bliss Merino DK: 100% wool. 110 yd/100 m per 1¾ oz (50 g) ball.

Elle True Blue DK: 100% cotton. 118 yd/108 m per 1¾ oz (50 g) ball.

Noro Kureyon: 100% wool. 110 yd/100 m per 1¾ oz (50 g) ball.

Patons Cotton 4 Ply: 100% cotton. 361 yd/330 m per 3½ oz (100 g) ball.

Patons Diploma Gold DK: 55% wool, 25% acrylic, 20% nylon. 131 yd/120 m per 1¾ oz (50 g) ball.

Rowan Big Wool: 100% merino wool. 87 yd/80 m per 3½ oz (100 g) ball.

Rowan Kidsilk Haze: 70% super kid mohair, 30% silk. 229 yd/210 m per 1 oz (25 g) ball.

Rowan Lurex Shimmer: 80% viscose, 20% polyester. 103 yd/95 m per 1 oz (25 g) ball.

Sirdar Bigga: 50% wool, 50% acrylic. 44 yd/40 m per 3½ oz (100 g) ball.

Sirdar Country Style DK: 45% acrylic, 40% nylon, 15% wool. 347 yd/318 m per 3½ oz (100 g) ball).

Sirdar Fresco: 100% nylon. 140 yd/128 m per 1¾ oz (50 g) ball.

Sirdar Funky Fur: 100% polyester. 98 yd/90 m per 1¾ oz (50 g) ball.

Sirdar Wow!: 100% polyester. 63 yd/58 m per 3½ oz (100 g) ball.

Sirdar Duet: 56% cotton, 44% nylon. 142 yd/130 m per 1¾ oz (50 g) ball.

Sirdar Yo-Yo: 74% acrylic, 14% wool, 12% polyester. 962 yd/880 m per 14 oz (400 g) ball.

Getting Started

FOLLOWING THE INSTRUCTIONS

Crochet instructions are really very easy to follow, once you familiarize yourself with the way they are set out. Before you start to crochet your garment, read through the instructions and make sure you understand what to expect. Make sure that you have the right yarn and a selection of crochet hooks. Check that you know what measurements you are working to – the 'to fit' sizes are provided as a guide but it is always a good idea to check that you will be happy with the actual finished measurements as the amount of ease varies according to the design. If in doubt about which size to make, compare the actual measurements with a garment you already have and like. Where instructions for different sizes are given, figures are given for the smallest size first and the larger sizes, separated by colons, follow in parentheses.

Abbreviations are used for many of the repetitive words that occur in crochet instructions. See above right for a list of the most frequently used abbreviations; any additional abbreviations will be given with each individual pattern.

Brackets are used where a set of instructions needs to be worked a number of times. For example: [3 tr in next ch sp] twice. This means that the instructions within the brackets are worked twice. Brackets can also be used to clarify working a group of stitches.

Stitch counts are also given at intervals throughout the pattern, often at the end of a row or round. These are set in brackets.

Asterisks are used to indicate repetition of a sequence of instructions.

READING STITCH DIAGRAMS

Where appropriate, stitch diagrams are also given. The stitch diagrams conform to the international symbols, with a few variations to explain individual stitches. The diagrams should be read in rows or in rounds exactly as the crochet is worked. Each stitch is represented by a symbol placed to create a picture of the stitch pattern, although occasionally symbols will have been stretched

ABBREVIATIONS			
beg	beg(inning)	rep	repeat
ch	chain	RS	right side
cont	continue	sc	single crochet
dc	double crochet	sp(s)	space(s)
dec	decreas(e)(ing)	sl st	slip stitch
dtr	double treble	st(s)	stitch(es)
foll	following	tog	together
hdc	half double crochet	tr	treble
inc	increas(e)(ing)	WS	wrong side
patt	pattern	yo	yarn over hook

or compressed for the sake of clarity. The purpose of the stitch diagrams is to provide a quick visual reference as it is often a lot easier to recognize that five bars across a T means wrap the yarn over the hook five times at the start of the stitch rather than trying to remember what 'quadtr' means. However, the written instructions are complete as they stand and all the projects can be completed without the stitch diagrams. Each stitch diagram will have a key: the standard symbols for the basic stitches are listed below:

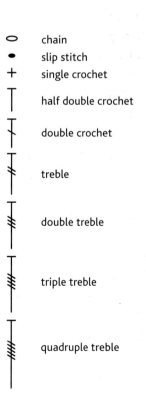

chain
slip stitch
single crochet
half double crochet
double crochet
treble
double treble
triple treble
quadruple treble

CHECKING YOUR GAUGE

Making sure that you have the correct gauge is extremely important as the finished item will look very different from the original if you don't get this right. Although each pattern states which hook size you should use, gauges can vary so it is intended as a guide only. Always change the hook size and try again if you do not achieve the gauge given. Gauges in crochet seem to vary a great deal, probably because the stitch size is governed equally by the gauge and tension of the yarn in your fingers and the size of the hook. You probably want to begin work on your garment but it is essential that you establish the correct gauge first by working up a sample.

In addition, the stitches at the edge of your work can distort, so it is best to check your gauge by working a few more stitches and rows than given for a 4-in (10-cm) square and then to count and mark the number of stitches and rows needed. Measure between markers or long pins. If you get more than 4 in (10 cm), your crochet is too loose. Try again using a smaller hook. If you get less than 4 in (10 cm), your work is too tight. Try again using a larger hook.

Basic techniques

MAKING A SLIP KNOT

Most projects start with a slip knot.

Make a loop in the yarn, about 6 in (15 cm) from the end. Insert the hook, catch the yarn and pull a loop through. Pull gently on both ends to tighten the knot and to close the loop on the hook.

HOLDING THE HOOK

Most hooks have a flattened area a little way down from the hooked end which helps you to find the best place for your fingers and makes the hook more comfortable to hold. You can hold the hook like a pencil with the rounded end above your hand or like a knife with the end under your hand. Most people find the pencil grip more flexible, so experiment to find which suits you. However you hold the hook, your grip should be light so you can easily move the hook in a forward and back motion.

HOLDING THE YARN AND THE WORK

Hold the tail end of yarn from the slip knot between first finger and thumb of your left hand. As the work grows, move the work to keep the thumb and first finger grip near the place that a new stitch will be made. The yarn lies over the middle and third fingers and is then wrapped around the little finger to control the tension. For extra control, to tighten a loose gauge or if working with fine or slippery yarns, wrap the yarn around the middle finger as well. Extending the middle finger lifts the yarn and makes it easy to catch the yarn with the hook.

CHAIN STITCH (ch)

Chain stitch may be used as a foundation for other stitches, to make spaces or arches between stitches or to reach the height of the other stitches when working in rounds or turning and working in rows.

With a slip knot on the hook, take the hook in front of the yarn, dip the tip to take the yarn over the hook from back to front and draw a new loop through the loop on the hook. Repeat for each chain stitch.

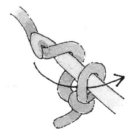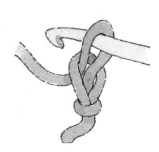

Here's a guide to the number of turning chains usually needed to give the correct height for some of the most often used stitches.

Single crochet	1 chain
Half double crochet	2 chains
Double crochet	3 chains
Treble	4 chains

SLIP STITCH (sl st)

Slip stitch is the shortest stitch. It's used for joining stitches or for carrying the yarn along an edge when shaping or to a new place in the stitch pattern. It helps to avoid having to fasten off and rejoin the yarn.

Insert the hook into a stitch, dip the tip of the hook to wrap the yarn over from back to front and draw a new loop through both the stitch and the loop on the hook, so that it ends with one loop on the hook. The steps show joining a length of chain in a ring but the action is the same when working into any stitch.

SINGLE CROCHET (sc)

Single crochet is like a slip stitch with an extra step. Depending on the yarn and hook size used, it can make a firm fabric when used alone. Single crochet can also be used with other stitches to link chains or to create stitch patterns. In this book, a single chain is worked at the start of each single crochet row but this chain is not worked into on the following row and it is not counted as a stitch. Some interesting variations on single crochet are Solomon's knot, crab stitch and loop stitch (see pages 13-14).

Insert the hook into the chain or stitch indicated in the instructions, dip the tip of the hook to wrap the yarn over from back to front and draw the yarn through the stitch to make two loops on the hook. Dip the tip of the hook to wrap the yarn over from back to front and draw the yarn through the two loops on the hook, so that it ends with one loop on the hook.

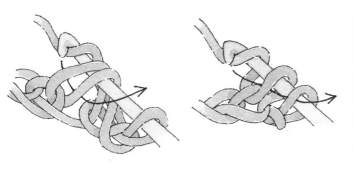

Tips

- *When working into the foundation chain, take the hook under two strands of each chain loop unless instructed otherwise.*
- *Wherever possible, join in new yarn at the start of a row, using the same method for changing colors.*
- *Try to work your foundation chain stitches quite loosely. If they are tight it will be difficult to work into them and the edge will pull in. To work an even, loose chain, try using a hook that is one or two sizes larger.*

DOUBLE CROCHET (dc)

Double crochet is like single crochet but with an extra step. It is probably the most frequently used stitch. When used alone, it makes a light, flexible fabric and it can be combined with other stitches in groups to create shells, clusters, mesh and openwork effects. Double crochet rows usually start with three chains to bring the yarn up to the height of the row. This counts as a stitch and the first stitch of the previous row is skipped to compensate. However, this can leave a gap between the first and second stitches so depending on the design, the first chain is often replaced with a single crochet worked directly into the first stitch.

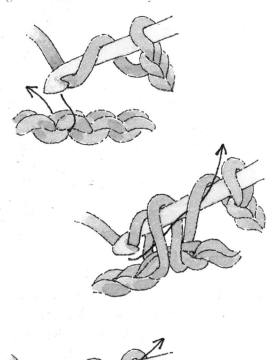

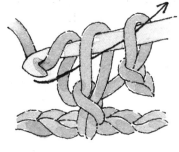

With the hook in front of the yarn, dip the tip of the hook to wrap the yarn over from back to front. Insert the hook into the chain or stitch indicated in the instructions. Dip the tip of the hook to wrap the yarn over from back to front and draw the yarn through the stitch to make three loops on the hook. Dip the tip of the hook to wrap the yarn over from back to front and draw the yarn through the first two loops on the hook. Wrap the yarn over the hook again and draw it through the two loops, so that it ends with one loop on the hook.

A half double crochet (hdc) is worked in the same way as a double crochet up to the second step as shown in the illustration at left, then the yarn is pulled through the new loop, the wrapped yarn, and the original loop all in one movement to make a stitch that's between single crochet and double crochet in height.

WORKING LONGER STITCHES

Treble (tr), double treble (dtr), triple treble (trtr), and quadruple treble (quadtr) are all worked in the same way as a double crochet but the stitches are made longer with one more wrapping of the yarn over the hook before you start, so that it requires one more step when drawing through the loops at the end. The symbols show an extra bar for each time you wrap the yarn over the hook. Different height stitches are often combined to create a petal shape.

Here's a guide for the number of times to wrap the yarn over the hook when making longer stitches.

Treble	twice
Double treble	three times
Triple treble	four times
Quadruple treble	five times

Variations on standard stitches

INSERTING THE HOOK

All the standard stitches are worked either under two strands of the starting chain or under both strands at the top of a stitch, however, there are variations in placing the hook which give different effects.

Inserting the hook into one strand only

This can be either at the front or at the back of the stitch. This can be used practically, when working into both sides of a starting chain or decoratively, to open up a fabric.

Inserting the hook between stitches

This opens up the fabric and may be quicker to work. It can be used if the fabric is too fine, or if it is difficult to insert the hook in a firm fabric. It can also be used to group more stitches together than would fit comfortably in a normal stitch.

Taking the hook around the post of a stitch

This is called a raised stitch because it lies on the surface of the work. Wrap the yarn over the hook as directed. Place the hook in front of the work and insert it down before the stitch designated in the row below. Then, bring it up after the stitch, completing the stitch in the usual way. Raised stitches can also be made on the back of the work.

Inserting the hook in the side of a stitch

This is particularly useful when making a single crochet or a double crochet chain. For a single crochet chain, make a slip knot and two chains. Insert the hook in the first chain and work one single crochet stitch. For each subsequent stitch, insert the hook under the threads at the side of the previous stitch. For a double crochet chain, make a slip knot and three chains. Take the yarn over the hook, then insert the hook into the third chain and complete the double crochet in the usual way. For each subsequent stitch, insert the hook under one or two of the strands at the bottom of the previous stitch. Single crochet and double crochet chains make more flexible edges than an ordinary starting chain. They are also easier to count.

the hook and pull through making a loose chain stitch. Insert hook in the back loop of the chain and work a single crochet stitch, this will lock the loose chain in place. Repeat and join knots as given in the instructions for the mohair wrap (page 104).

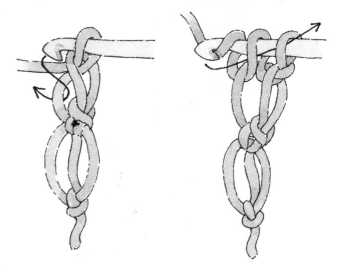

Variations on single crochet

SOLOMON'S KNOT

This stitch is simply a chain stitch, elongated and secured with a single crochet stitch.

Pull up loop to length required, take the yarn over

CRAB STITCH (OR REVERSE SINGLE CROCHET)

This is an excellent edging stitch. It is literally single crochet, worked backwards. It is best worked after a right side row of single crochet.

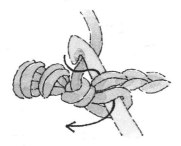

Do not turn the work at the end of the row. Instead, insert the hook in the previous stitch, take the yarn over the hook and pull it through to make two loops on the hook. Take the yarn over the hook again and pull it through so that one loop remains on the hook. Repeat this sequence along the edge. Crab stitch spreads the edge slightly so there's no need to increase at corners. If the edge flutes, either skip the occasional stitch in the single crochet row or use a smaller hook.

LOOP STITCH

This is really a single crochet stitch with the middle loop pulled out and locked with another stitch. It is always worked on wrong side rows, so the loop, which is made at the back of the work, appears on the right side.

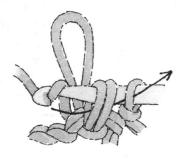

Insert the hook. Extend the middle finger to form a loop. Take both threads of the loop over the hook and pull through to make three loops on the hook. Take the yarn over the hook. Pull it through the three loops on the hook and remove your finger from the loop. (Keeping the middle finger of the left hand extended can be tiring. You may find it easier to transfer the extended loop to the right hand after pulling through to make three loops on the hook.)

Grouping stitches

Stitches of any length can be grouped or worked together to increase or decrease the number of stitches in a row or to create a decorative effect. If complete stitches are worked into the same stitch, a shell or increase is made. Or, they can be linked at the top to create a popcorn. If the stitches are worked in a row but joined at the top, a cluster or decrease is made. Working stitches all in the same place and joining them at the top makes a bobble.

SHELL / INCREASE

Working two or more complete stitches into the same stitch in the row below can increase the number of stitches in a row or be used to make a shell stitch pattern.

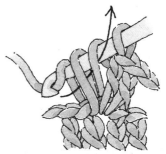

This illustration shows three double crochet stitches all worked into one double crochet in the row below. Simply work the double crochet stitches in the usual way but insert the hook in the same stitch each time. Because the stitches are held together at the bottom, not the top, working more than two or three stitches in the same place will form a shell shape.

CLUSTER / DECREASE

Any combination of stitches can be joined together at the top by leaving the last loop of each stitch on the hook, then working all the loops together to complete the cluster. Clustering two or three stitches together can also be a way of decreasing.

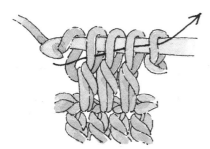

This illustration shows how three stitches can be clustered together. Leaving the last loop of each stitch on the hook, work a double crochet into each of the next three stitches, therefore making four loops on the hook. Take the yarn over the hook and pull through all four loops to join the stitches together at the top.

BOBBLE

When a cluster is worked into one stitch, a bobble is made. If the stitches used for the bobble are longer than the background stitches, the bobble will stand away from the surface.

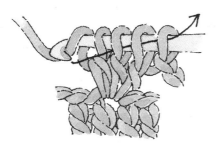

This illustration shows three double crochet stitches worked together. Wrap the yarn over the hook and insert the hook into the stitch. Take the yarn over the hook and pull it through. Do not complete the double crochet. Leave this last loop on the hook and continue working part double crochet stitches, each time leaving one more loop on the hook, until there are four loops on the hook including the original loop. Take the yarn over the hook and pull it through all four loops.

BASIC INFORMATION

POPCORN

This method makes a bobble that stands up from the surface without the need to make longer stitches. A popcorn can be placed in any stitch and be made up of any practical number or combination of stitches.

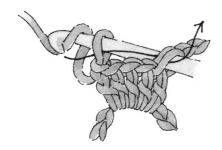

This illustration shows a five-double crochet popcorn worked into a chain space. Inserting a hook in the same place each time, work five double crochet stitches. Lengthen the last loop slightly and slip out the hook. Insert the hook into the top of the first stitch, then into the last loop. Take the yarn over the hook and pull it through, tightening the stitch to make the popcorn stand up.

MAKING GARMENTS

WORKING IN ROWS

The fabric usually starts with a foundation chain, a single or double crochet chain or a picot row. Each row of the instructions will tell you where to place the hook and which stitch to work. Simply turn the work at the end of each row so the right and wrong side face alternately. The instructions will tell you how many turning chains to work or how to deal with the edge stitches.

WORKING IN ROUNDS

The fabric is worked from the center outward. The starting point can be a ring of chain or a loop ring. Chain gives a very firm start. Loop rings can be neater and less obtrusive. A loop ring is made by working into yarn wound once around the left index finger. The free end is worked over and pulled gently to close the ring when the first round of stitches has been completed.

When working in rounds, the right side always faces you. The instructions will tell you how to join at the end of each round and how many chains to work to match the height of the stitches in the next round.

COLOR CROCHET

Capital letters, A, B, C etc are used to designate the different colors. Because the last loop of a stitch forms the top of the next stitch, when changing colors, work the last stitch in the old color until two loops remain on the hook, then use the new color to complete the stitch. For some striped color patterns, you can carry the yarn not in use up the side of the work. If this is not practical, cut the yarn and work over the ends. When working color motifs, carry the yarn not in use along and slightly behind the top of the stitches in the row below and work over it until needed.

FINISHING

Some of the designs are worked in the round, so there is a minimum of finishing to do. Garments worked in flat pieces can be sewn together or joined using crochet. Placing markers and pinning seams will help to match the rows and give a neater finish. If sewing, preferably, join the pieces with the right sides facing, matching the rows and taking in two threads of each stitch from each side rather than whole stitches to reduce the bulk. Alternatively, place the right sides together and oversew the seams.

Joining a seam with crochet gives a firm, neat chain edge. Insert the hook under an edge stitch from each side and work a slip stitch or a single crochet stitch. The instructions will tell you if the crocheted seams are intended to be decorative and should be worked with the right side facing out. If the ball band states the yarn can be pressed, press the pieces, checking that they are the correct size. Press again after joining the shoulders and setting in the sleeves.

CLASSIC

From classics with a vintage twist to modern classics, the clothes in this section will always be in style. You'll find projects to suit every look, from the generously sized denim duffle – which will be even better when worn and weathered – to the glamorous chic of a thirties-style boa which takes just a few hours to make. In between there are new looks for old favorites, the brightest scarf with a chevron pattern, a patterned hat, a glorious poncho, and a cropped zip-up jacket. Invest the time in creating these clever classics and you'll wear them time and time again.

This casual coat with a softly draped hood is a classic that will become a wardrobe staple. Worked in a cotton yarn dyed pure indigo, the coat will fade when washed, revealing the intricate texture of the stitches.

DENIM DUFFLE COAT

★☆☆ BEGINNER

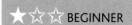 *When working even, the instructions give 1 sc and 2 ch at the beginning of a row instead of the usual 3 ch to help close the gap between the first and second stitches. The sc and 2 ch is counted as one stitch. When increasing, 3 turning chains are worked and a dc is worked into the first tr, therefore making one stitch.*

Because it can be difficult to work the starting chain loosely even if you use a larger hook, the back and fronts are worked from the top downward so the lower edge cannot pull in. The sleeves are worked from the cuff upward so the softer finishing edge is at the top.

HELPFUL HINTS
- For a jacket without a hood you'll need approximately three less balls of yarn.
- When making a lot of chain, it can be difficult to count the stitches. If in doubt, add a few extra stitches, it's easier to undo spare chain than to undo the first row to add more chain if you've miscounted.
- Elle True Blue is a 100% cotton indigo dyed yarn that is made to fade and shrinks by approximately 5% in length in the first wash. The measurements and tension given are for before washing.

MEASUREMENTS

To fit bust

34–36	38–40	42–44	46–48	in
86–91	97–102	107–112	117–122	cm

Actual bust

45¼	49¼	53	57	in
115	125	135	145	cm

Actual length

27½	27½	32½	32½	in
70	70	83	83	cm

Actual sleeve

20 in
51 cm

In the instructions, figures are given for the smallest size first; larger sizes follow in parentheses. Where only one set of figures is given this applies to all sizes.

MATERIALS
- 19 (21:24:26) × 50 g balls of Elle True Blue DK in Denim 112
- F/5 (3.75 mm) crochet hook
- 4 toggles

GAUGE
16 sts and 9 rows to 4 in (10 cm) measured over double crochet before washing using F/5 (3.75 mm) hook. Change hook size if necessary to obtain this gauge.

ABBREVIATIONS
MB (make bobble) – leaving last loop of each st on hook, work 5 tr all in same st, yo and pull through all 6 loops on hook
2dctog – leaving last loop of each st on hook, work 1 dc in each of next 2 sts, yo and pull though 3 loops on hook
See also page 9.

DUFFLE COAT

BOBBLE DIAMOND PANEL
Worked over 17 sts.
Row 1 (WS): MB, 1 dc in each of next 15 dc, MB.
Row 2 and every RS row: 1 dc in each of next 17 sts.
Row 3: MB, [1 dc in each of next 7 dc, MB] twice.

Key:

dc

MB

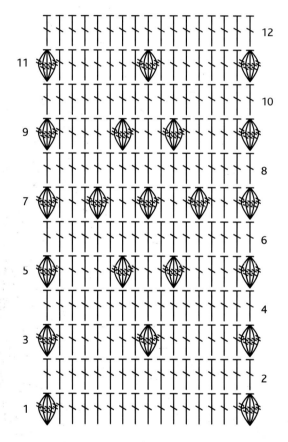

Because the sleeve increases are on every 3rd row, they alternate between RS and WS rows but as the stitch pattern is the same on every row, the increases are made in the same way. Mark each increase row with a contrasting loop of yarn to make it easier to keep track of them and also to make it easier to match the rows when sewing the seam.

Row 5: MB, 1 dc in each of next 5 dc, MB, 1 dc in each of next 3 dc, MB, 1 dc in each of next 5 dc, MB.
Row 7: MB, [1 dc in each of next 3 dc, MB] 4 times.
Row 9: As Row 5.
Row 11: As Row 3.
Row 12: As Row 2.
Repeat these 12 rows for bobble diamond panel patt.

RIGHT FRONT
Make 33 (37:39:43) ch.

Shape neck
Row 1 (WS): 1 dc in 4th ch from hook, 1 dc in each ch to end. [31 (35:37:41) sts.]
Row 2: 1 sc in 1st dc, 2 ch, 1 dc in each dc to last st, 1 dc in 3rd ch **.
Row 3: 1 sc in 1st dc, 2 ch, 1 dc in each of next 2 (4:4:6) dc, work 17 sts of Row 1 of bobble diamond panel, 1 dc in each of next 10 (12:14:16) dc, 1 dc in 2nd ch.
Row 4: 1 sc in 1st dc, 2 ch, 1 dc in each st to last st, 2 dc in 2nd ch. [32 (36:38:42) sts.]
Row 5: 3 ch, 1 dc in 1st dc, 1 dc in each of next 3 (5:5:7) dc, work 17 sts of Row 3 of bobble diamond panel, 1 dc in each dc to last st, 1 dc in 2nd ch. [33 (37:39:43) sts.]
Cont in dc with bobble diamond panel as set, inc at neck edge in same way as Rows 4 and 5 on next 5 (5:7:7) rows, so ending with a RS row. [38 (42:46:50) sts.]

Shape front neck
Do not turn after last row, make 12 ch, turn.
Next row (WS): 1 dc in 4th ch from hook, 1 dc in each of next 8 ch, patt to end. [48 (52:56:60) sts.]
Cont working bobble diamond panel patt with dc at each side for 52 (52:62:62) more rows, so ending with Row 1 of 6th (6th:7th:7th) bobble diamond panel patt. Fasten off.

LEFT FRONT

Work as right front to **.

Row 3 (WS): 1 sc in 1st dc, 2 ch, 1 dc in each of next 10 (12:14:16) dc, work 17 sts of Row 1 of bobble diamond panel, 1 dc in each of next 2 (4:4:6) dc, 1 dc in 2nd ch.

Row 4: 3 ch, 1 dc in 1st dc, 1 dc in each st to last st, 1 dc in 2nd ch.
[32 (36:38:42) sts.]

Row 5: 1 sc in 1st dc, 2 ch, 1 dc in each of next 10 (12:14:16) dc, work 17 sts of Row 3 of bobble diamond panel, 1 dc in each of next 3 (5:5:7) dc, 2 dc in 3rd ch.
[33 (37:39:43) sts.]

Cont in dc with bobble diamond panel as set, inc at neck edge in same way as Rows 4 and 5 on next 5 (5:7:7) rows, so ending with a RS row. [38 (42:46:50) sts.]

Shape front neck

Join a spare length of yarn at neck edge and make 10 ch.

Next row (WS): 1 sc in 1st dc, 2 ch, patt to 10 ch, 1 dc in each of 10 ch.
[48 (52:56:60) sts.]

Cont working bobble diamond panel patt with dc at each side for 52 (52:62:62) more rows, so ending with Row 1 of 6th (6th:7th:7th) bobble diamond panel patt. Fasten off.

BACK

Make 94 (102:110:118) ch.

Row 1 (WS): 1 dc in 4th ch from hook, 1 dc in each ch to end. [92 (100:108:116) sts.]

Row 2: 1 sc in 1st dc, 2 ch, 1 dc in each dc to last st, 1 dc in 3rd ch.

Row 2 forms dc patt. Working into 2nd ch for last st on foll rows, cont in dc for 61 (61:73:73) more rows. Fasten off.

SLEEVES (MAKE 2)

Make 50 (54:58:62) ch.

Row 1 (RS): 1 dc in 4th ch from hook, 1 dc in each ch to end. [48 (52:56:60) sts.]

Row 2: 1 sc in 1st dc, 2 ch, 1 dc in each dc to last st, 1 dc in 3rd ch.

Cont in dc patt as given for back, work 1 row.

Inc row: 3 ch, 1 dc in 1st dc, 1 dc in each dc to last st, 2 dc in 2nd ch. [50 (54:58:62) sts.]

Cont in dc, inc in this way at each end of 13 foll 3rd rows. [76 (80:84:88) sts.]

Work 3 rows. Fasten off.

HOOD

Front

Make 131 (131:135:135) ch.

Row 1 (RS): 1 dc in 4th ch from hook, 1 dc in each ch to end. [129 (129:133:133) sts.]

Cont in dc patt as given for back, work 2 rows.

Dec row: 1 sc in 1st dc, 2 ch, 2dctog, 1 dc in each dc to last 3 sts, 2dctog, 1 dc in 2nd ch. [127 (127:131:131) sts.]

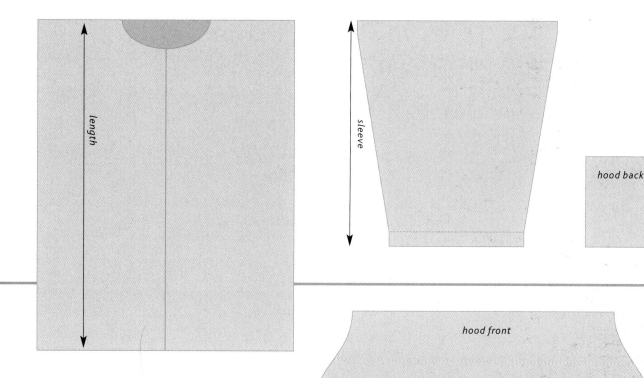

length

sleeve

hood back

hood front

Cont in dc, dec in this way at each end of next 11 (11:13:13) rows. [105 sts.] Work 3 (3:4:5) rows. Fasten off.

Back

Make 29 ch.

Row 1 (RS): 1 dc in 4th ch from hook, 1 dc in each ch to end. [27 sts.]

Cont in dc, work 19 more rows. Fasten off.

TOGGLE LOOPS (MAKE 8)

Make 31 ch.

Row 1: 1 sc in 2nd ch from hook, 1 sc in each ch to end. [30 sts.] Fasten off.

FRONT AND NECK EDGING

With WS together and back facing, matching sts, join right shoulder seam with sc. With WS together and back facing, join left shoulder seam in the same way. With RS facing, join yarn at right front lower edge.

Row 1 (RS): Work 106 (106:130:130) sc in row ends to right front neck, 30 (30:34:34) sc up right front neck, 30 (30:34:34) sc across back neck, 30 (30:34:34) sc down left front neck and 106 (106:130:130) sc in row ends down left front edge.

Row 2: 1 ch, 1 sc in each dc to left front neck, 2 sc in next sc, 1 sc in each sc to last sc around neck, 2 sc in next sc, 1 sc in each sc to end. Fasten off.

FINISHING

Join all seams with a row of sc to make a ridge on RS.

Place markers 9½ (9¾:10½:10¾) in (24 (25:26.5:27.5) cm) down from shoulders on back and fronts. Join sleeves between markers. Set back of hood into shorter edge of front of hood. Noting that seams of back of hood do not join to shoulder seams, join shaped edge of hood to neck edge. Join side and sleeve seams, reversing seam for turn back cuffs. Knot ends of toggle loops to make a neat bobble with a loop at folded end. Sew four loops on each front. Enclose a toggle in each loop on left front and stitch to secure.

This hat is worked in the round from the top down. The earflaps are worked in rows but are worked so that the single crochet fabric look the same as the rest of the hat.

INCA-STYLE EARFLAP HAT

★★☆ MEDIUM

 *Color patterned crochet is easier to work in rounds because the yarn ends are always on the wrong side.*

Changing color to work the patterns is easier because the right side of the hat is always facing.

HELPFUL HINTS
- The hat is worked from the top down.
- Single crochet in rounds has a different appearance than single crochet worked in rows. To work a gauge square, use the method of working rows that are all worked in the same direction as used for the earflaps, or start the top of the hat and measure from the center to the edge after 11 rounds. If this measures 2½ in (6 cm) and the circumference is 12½ in (31.5 cm), you can continue; if it is larger start again using a smaller hook, if it is smaller start again using a larger hook.
- Simply work over the yarn not in use to carry it along until needed.
- As a general rule, while increasing, change to B for last loop of last st in A but do not change A before completing last st of motif in B. When working even, change color for the last loop each time.
- Do not count the 1 ch at the beginning of the round as a stitch. Always work the first sc in the same place as the sl st of the previous round.

MEASUREMENTS
Finished circumference
23 in
58.5 cm

MATERIALS
- 2 × 50 g balls of Debbie Bliss Cotton Cashmere in Blue 12 (A)
- 1 × 50 g ball of Debbie Bliss Cotton Cashmere in Pink 19 (B)
- E/4 (3.50 mm) crochet hook

GAUGE
19 sts and 20 rows to 4 in (10 cm) measured over single crochet worked in rounds using E/4 (3.50 mm) hook. Change hook size if necessary to obtain this gauge.

ABBREVIATIONS
2sctog – insert hook in first st, yo and pull through, insert hook in second st, yo and pull through, yo and pull through 3 loops on hook *See also page 9.*

EARFLAP HAT

HAT
Wind A around finger to make a ring, insert hook and pull loop through.
Round 1 (RS): 3 ch, 11 dc in ring, pull end to close ring, sl st in 3rd ch. [12 sts.]
Round 2: 1 ch, 1 sc in 3rd ch, 1 sc in each dc, sl st in 1st sc. [12 sts.]
Round 3: Using A, work 1 ch, 2 sc in same place as ss, 2 sc in next sc, [2scB in next sc, 2scA in each of foll 2 sc] 3 times, 2scB in next sc, sl st in 1st sc. [24 sts.]

TIP

To make a tassel with a nice round top, tie the strands of yarn in the center and fold them in half. Then insert a few of the inner strands into the hole in a large wooden bead, and slide the bead to the bottom of the tassel. Conceal the bead, arranging the other strands around the bead before wrapping the tie thread around the base of the bead and securing the end.

Round 4: 1chA, [1scA in each of 3 sc, 2scB in next sc, 1scB in foll sc, 2scB in next sc] 4 times, sl st in 1st sc. [32 sts.]

Round 5: 1chA, [1scA in each of 2sc, 2scB in next sc, 1scB in each of foll 4 sc, 2scB in next sc] 4 times, sl st in 1st sc. [40 sts.]

Round 6: 1chB, 1scB in each of 5 sc, [2scA in next sc, 1scB in each of 9 sc] 3 times, 2scA in next sc, 1scB in each of 4 sc, sl st in 1st sc. [44 sts.]

Round 7: 1chB, 1scB in each of 4 sc, [1scA in each of next 5 sc, 1scB in each of 6 sc] 3 times, 1scA in each of next 5 sc, 1scB in each of 2 sc, sl st in 1st sc.

Round 8: 1chB, 1scB in each of 3 sc, [1scA in each of next 7 sc, 1scB in each of 4 sc] 3 times, 1scA in each of next 7 sc, 1scB in last sc, sl st in 1st sc.

Round 9: 1chB, 1scB in each of 2 sc, [* 2scA in each of next 2 sc, 1scA in each of foll 5 sc, 2scA in each of next 2 sc *, 1scB in each of 2 sc] 3 times, rep from * to *, sl st in 1st sc. [60 sts.]

Rounds 10 and 11: Using A, work 2 rounds.

Round 12: Using B, 1 ch, [1 sc in each of next 5 sc, 2 sc in foll sc] 10 times, sl st in 1st sc. [70 sts.]

Round 13: Using B, work 1 round.

Rounds 14, 15, 16 and 17: Work 4 rounds from Chart 1.

Round 18: Using A, 1 ch, 2 sc in 1st sc, [1 sc in each of next 4 sc, 2 sc in next sc] to last 4 sc, 1 sc in each sc, sl st in 1st sc. [84 sts.]

Round 19: Using A, work 1 round.

Round 20: Using B, work 1 round.

Round 21: Using B, 1 ch, [1scB, 1scA] to end.

Rounds 22 and 23: Using A, work 2 rounds.

Round 24: Using A, 1 ch, [1 sc in each of next 6 sc, 2 sc in foll sc] 12 times, sl st in 1st sc. [96 sts.]

Round 25: Using A, work 1 round.

Round 26: Using B, work 1 round.

Round 27: As round 21.

Round 28: Using A, work 1 round.

Round 29: Using A, 1 ch, [1 sc in each of next 5 sc, 2 sc in foll sc] 16 times, sl st in 1st sc. [112 sts.]

Round 30: Using A, work 1 round.

Rounds 31 to 40: Work 10 rounds from Chart 2.

Rounds 41 to 43: Using A, work 3 rounds. Fasten off.

RIGHT EARFLAP

Using A, join yarn in 14th sc from beg of round. 1 ch, 1 sc same sc as joined yarn, 1 sc in each of next 19 sc, fasten off by enlarging last loop, passing the ball of yarn through it and pulling yarn to close loop. [20 sts.] Lay the yarn along the edge of the work and join in first stitch.

Next row (RS): 1 ch, working over yarn, work 1 sc in each sc to end, fasten off as before.

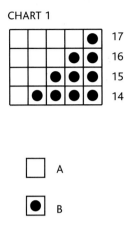

CHART 1

					●	17
			●	●		16
		●	●	●		15
	●	●	●	●		14

☐ A

■ B

CHART 2

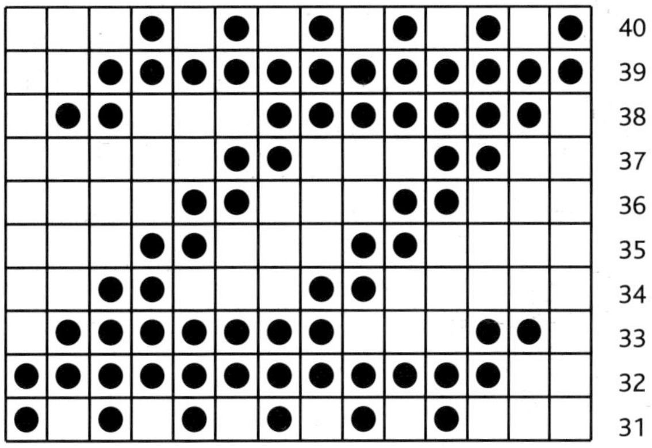

(rows 31–40)

Cont in sc fastening off at end of each row and working over yarn so RS is always facing, work 1 more row.

Dec row (RS): 1 ch, skip 1st sc, 1 sc in each sc to last 2 sc, 2sctog. [18 sts.]

Cont in RS sc, dec in this way at each end of 3 foll 3rd rows, then at each end of next 3 rows. [6 sts.] Fasten off.

LEFT EARFLAP

Skip center 46 sc, join A in next sc and work as given for Right Earflap.

EDGING

Join yarn A at beg of last round and work 1 round sc all around edge of hat.

Next round: Work as Round 21.

Next round: Using B work 1 round sc. Turn at end of round.

Next round: Using B and working 3sctog at each side of earflap to keep flaps flat, work 1 round sc. Fasten off.

FINISHING

Make a tassel using twenty-four 12-in (30-cm) long strands of B. Sew on top of hat.

VARIATION

ONE COLOR HAT

If you want the hat in just one color, simply follow the shaping as given but use just one color, ignoring the color changes and working the chart pattern rounds plain. You'll still need three balls of Debbie Bliss Cotton Cashmere in the color of your choice.

To work from charts, work in sc reading every line of chart from right to left.

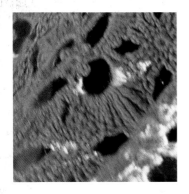

A quartet of leaf shapes form pretty floral motifs on this elegant poncho. Understated when worn off the shoulder and paired with casual slacks, the poncho can as easily be worn with a skirt or dress for a more dramatic look.

LEAF MOTIF PONCHO

 *The poncho is made from 4-leaf motifs joined to form a square with the four motifs at the center omitted to make the neck hole.*

Instructions are given for making and joining all of the leaf motif blocks, then working all the filler motifs. If you prefer, you can work the filler motifs as you join the blocks.

You can work over the end of the 8-ch ring at the center of the leaf motif block for a few stitches, then just snip it off. However, the end of each filler motif should be securely woven in before trimming.

HELPFUL HINTS

- Using different height stitches makes Round 3 of the motif grow really quickly. Here's a reminder of how many times to take the yarn over the hook before inserting the hook to work the stitches: sc = zero times, hdc = once but pull through all loops first time; dc = once; tr = twice, dtr = 3 times; trtr = 4 times, quadtr = 5 times.
- Save finishing time by weaving in the ends as you join motifs.

MEASUREMENTS

One size
Actual width
40 in
102 cm
Actual length (from shoulder to point)
28¼ in
72 cm

MATERIALS

- 13 × 50 g balls of Patons Diploma Gold DK in Apple Green 06125
- F/5 (3.75 mm) crochet hook

GAUGE

One leaf block measures 5 × 5 in (12.5 cm × 12.5 cm) when pressed, using F/5 (3.75 mm) hook. Change hook size if necessary to obtain this gauge.

ABBREVIATIONS

trtr – triple treble
quadtr – quadruple treble
See also page 9.

PONCHO

LEAF MOTIF BLOCK

Make 8 ch, sl st in 1st ch to form a ring.
Round 1 (RS): 7 ch, [2 sc in ring, 6 ch] 7 times, 2 sc in ring, sl st in 1st ch, sl st in each of next 2 ch.
Round 2: 1 ch, 2 sc in 1st 7-ch loop, [16 ch, skip next 6-ch loop, 3 sc in next 6-ch loop] 3 times, 16 ch, 1 sc in 1st 6-ch loop, sl st in 1st sc.
Round 3: Work [2 sc, 2 hdc, 2 dc, 2 tr, 2 dtr, 2 trtr, 1 quadtr, 2 trtr, 2 dtr, 2 tr, 2 dc, 2 hdc, 2 sc] in each 16-ch loop.
Round 4: * Sl st in each of next 2 sc, [4 ch, sl st in each of next 2 sts] 11 times, sl st in last sc of leaf, rep from * 3 more times, sl st in 1st sl st. Fasten off.

1st line of blocks, second motif

Work as first motif to Round 4.
Round 4: * Sl st in each of next 2 sc, [4 ch, sl st in each of next 2 sts] 11 times, sl st in last sc of leaf, rep from * once more, ** sl st in each of next 2 sc, [4 ch, sl st in each of next 2 sts] 5 times, with WS together join to 6th 4-ch loop at point of leaf of previous motif by

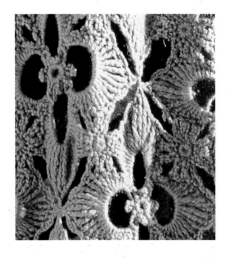
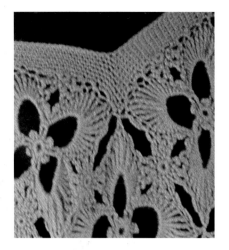
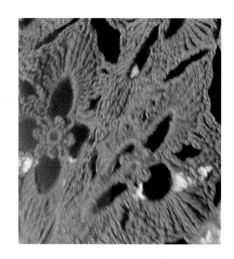

working 2 ch, sc in 4-ch loop, 2 ch, sl st in each of next 2 sts, [4 ch, sl st in each of next 2 sts] 5 times, sl st in last sc of leaf, rep from ** once more, joining in 4-ch loop of next leaf of previous motif, sl st in 1st sl st. Fasten off. Continue making and joining blocks in this way until 1st line of 8 blocks has been completed.

2nd and 3rd lines of blocks

Join 8 blocks in the same way but linking blocks to 4-ch loops of previous row as well as to each other.

4th and 5th lines of blocks

Join 3 blocks, omit center two blocks, join 3 blocks.

6th, 7th and 8th lines of blocks

Join as 2nd line of blocks.

BLOCK FILLER MOTIFS

Worked into center three 4-ch sps of each of 4 leaves of adjacent blocks.

Loop yarn around first finger to make a ring.

Round 1 (RS): 1 ch, 12 sc in ring, pull end to close ring, sl st in 1st sc.

Round 2: 2 ch, * 1 sc in 2nd 4-ch sp of 1st leaf, [2 ch, sl st in next sc of 1st round, 2 ch, 1 sc in next 4-ch sp] twice, 2 ch, sl st in next sc of 1st round, rep from * working into center three 4-ch sps of each of next 3 leaves,

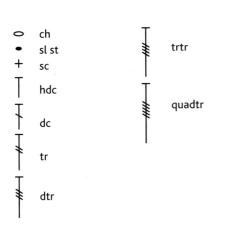

○ ch	
● sl st	
+ sc	─┼─ trtr
│ hdc	
│ dc	═╪═ quadtr
╪ tr	
╪ dtr	

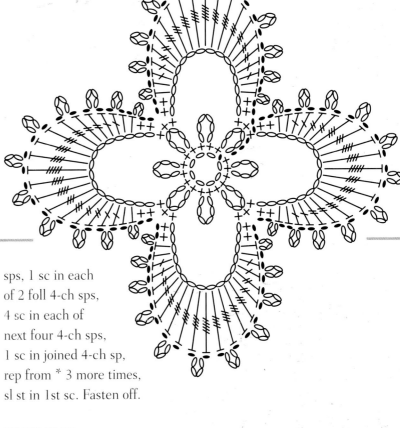

ending sl st in 1st sc of 1st round. Fasten off. Work a filler motif in each space between blocks.

NECK FILLER MOTIFS

Work in same way as block filler motif but make only 9 sc in ring on 1st round and join into 2 leaves of motif only.

NECKBAND

With RS facing, join yarn in a joined 4-ch sp at one corner of neck.

Round 1 (RS): 1 ch, [2 sc in 1st ch sp of block, 3 sc in each of next 3 ch sps, 1 sc in each of next 3 sc of filler motif, 3 sc in each of next 3 ch sps, 2 sc in foll ch sp] 8 times, sl st in 1st sc. [200 sts.] Skipping 1st sc, 2 sc at each corner and last sc on each round, work 7 rounds sc. [144 sts.] Fasten off.

EDGING

With RS facing, join yarn in joined 4ch sp of 2nd block along from one corner of outer edge of poncho.

Round 1 (RS): 1 ch, * [1 sc in joined 4-ch sp, 4 sc in each of next four 4-ch sps, 1 sc in each of 2 foll 4-ch sps, 4 sc in each of next four 4-ch sps, 1 sc in joined 4-ch sp] 6 times, 1 sc in joined 4-ch sp, 4 sc in each of next four 4-ch sps, 1 sc in each of 2 foll 4-ch sps, 4 sc in each of next four 4-ch sps, 7 sc in corner 4-ch sp, 4 sc in each of next four 4-ch

sps, 1 sc in each of 2 foll 4-ch sps, 4 sc in each of next four 4-ch sps, 1 sc in joined 4-ch sp, rep from * 3 more times, sl st in 1st sc. Fasten off.

FINISHING

Press according to ball band. Darn in ends.

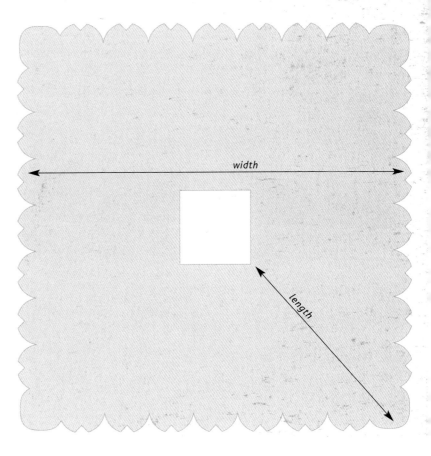

The vibrant zigzag pattern of this extra-long scarf is emphasized by brilliant color changes, made possible by increasing and decreasing the stitches at regular intervals in double crochet.

LONG ZIGZAG SCARF

★☆☆ **BEGINNER**

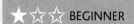 *You'll find it easy to follow the color changes if you cut snippets of the yarn and stick them down in the order given on a spare piece of paper. This will allow you to see at a glance which color to use next.*

The scarf starts with a double crochet chain rather than the basic foundation chain because a double crochet chain gives a more flexible edge and is a lot easier to work into for the first row.

The starting chain is a multiple of 16 plus 1, the pattern is a multiple of 17 plus 1.

HELPFUL HINTS

- If you don't want to do double crochet chain, you can work the same number of basic foundation chain very loosely, plus three chain to count as the first stitch, then work an extra row in A.
- When changing colors, work the last loop of the last stitch of the row in the next color.
- Cut the yarn and work over the ends each time you change colors. Do not carry yarns up the side of the work, as they will show. Make sure that the worked over ends lie on top of stitches of the same color. For single row stripes, weave the new end in as you work the 3 ch, then work over the tail of the yarn at the end of the next row.

MEASUREMENTS

10 × 86½ in
25.5 × 194 cm

MATERIALS

- 2 × 50 g balls of Patons Diploma Gold DK in each of the following: Berry 06129 (A), Hot Pink 06247 (B), Honey 06228 (D), Ginger 06211 (E) and Jaffa 06252 (F)
- 1 × 50 g ball of Patons Diploma Gold DK in Red 06151 (C)
- F/5 (3.75 mm) crochet hook

GAUGE

17 sts measure 3⅜ in (8.5 cm), 9 rows to 4 in (10 cm) over chevron pattern using F/5 (3.75 mm) hook. Change hook size if necessary to obtain this gauge.

ABBREVIATIONS

See page 9.

SCARF

Double crochet chain: Using A, make a slip knot and work 3 ch, 1 dc in 3rd ch from hook, * inserting hook under two strands at bottom left of previous dc, work 1 dc in previous dc, rep from * until there are 49 sts.

Row 1 (RS): 3 ch, 1 dc in 1st dc, [1 dc in each of next 7 dc, skip 1 dc, 1 dc in each of next 7 dc, 3 dc in next dc] twice, 1 dc in each of next 7 dc, skip 1 dc, 1 dc in each of next 7 dc, 2 dc in last st. [52 sts.] Change to B.

Row 2: 3 ch, 1 dc in 1st dc, [1 dc in each of next 7 dc, skip 2 dc, 1 dc in each of next 7 dc, 3 dc in next dc] twice, 1 dc in each of next 7 dc, skip 2 dc, 1 dc in each of next 7 dc, 2 dc in last st.

Row 2 forms the chevron patt.

Work 2 more rows B, 1 row A, 1 row B.

First 7-row repeat has been completed.

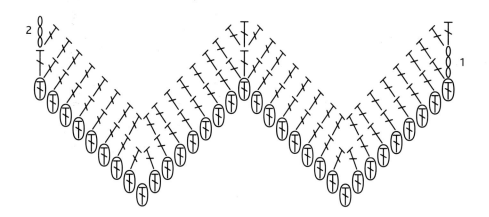

◯	ch
⊕	dcch
┼	dc

Work in stripe pattern as follows:
2 rows C, 3 rows D, 1 row C, 1 row D,
2 rows E, 3 rows F, 1 row E, 1 row F,
2 rows C, 3 rows A, 1 row C, 1 row A,
2 rows B, 3 rows F, 1 row B, 1 row F,
2 rows D, 3 rows E, 1 row D, 1 row E,
2 rows A, 3 rows B, 1 row A, 1 row B.
These 42 rows form the stripe patt.
Work last 42 rows 3 more times. Fasten off.

VARIATION

ONE-COLOR SCARF

The chevron pattern will create an interesting texture if you make the scarf in just one color. For a scarf the same size as the main project, you will need 7 × 50 g balls of Patons Diploma Gold DK.

Using just two easy-to-work square motifs, the color tones in this vest are mixed and matched to create a dynamic pattern. Panels on each side of the vest give it a shaped fit.

PATCHWORK SQUARES VEST

HELPFUL HINTS

- This is an ideal project to carry around with you so you can work a square whenever you have a few spare moments.
- Post stitches and popcorns add textural interest to the motifs.

MEASUREMENTS

To fit bust

32–34	36–38	40–42	in
81–86	91–97	102–107	cm

Actual width

33½	37¾	41	in
85	96	104	cm

Actual length

25½ in
65 cm

In the instructions, figures are given for the smallest size first; larger sizes follow in parentheses. Where only one set of figures is given this applies to all sizes.

MATERIALS

- 2 × 100 g balls of Sirdar Country Style DK in each of Parchment 404 (A), Chocolate 530 (B) and Cream 411 (C)
- 3 buttons
- E/4 (3.50 mm) crochet hook

GAUGE

Each motif measures 3⅛ in (8 cm) square, 22 sts and 9 rows to 4 in (10 cm) over double crochet both using E/4 (3.50 mm) hook. Change hook size if necessary to obtain this gauge.

ABBREVIATIONS

PC (popcorn) – work 3 dc in same st, remove hook from working loop and insert in top of first dc, pick up working loop, draw through and work 1 ch to close popcorn

Fpdc (front post double crochet) – take yarn twice over hook, insert hook from right to left around post of dc one row below, yo and draw loop through, [yo and pull through 2 loops] 3 times

2dctog – leaving last loop of each st on hook, work 1tr in each of next 2 sts, yo and pull through 3 loops on hook
See also page 9.

NOTE

Make 29 of each of the flower and square motifs and one of each half motif.
A, B and C are given for the first square in each motif, change colors to work five of each motif in ABC, ACB, BAC, BCA, CAB and four in CBA.

After changing colors, work over the ends to save time weaving in.

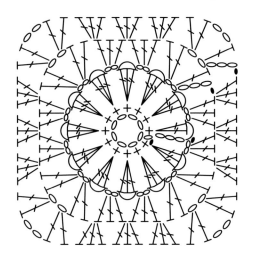
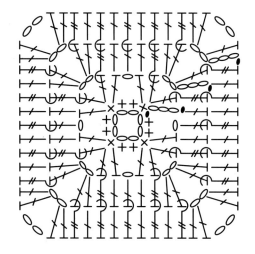
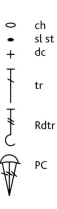

	ch
	sl st
	dc
	tr
	Rdtr
	PC

VEST

FLOWER MOTIF

Using A, make 8 ch, sl st in 1st ch to form a ring.

Round 1 (RS): 1 ch, 12 sc in ring, sl st in 1st sc.

Round 2: 3 ch, 2 dc in same place as sl st, remove hook, insert in 3rd ch, pick up working loop, draw through and work 1 ch to close 1st popcorn, [2 ch, 1 PC in next sc] 11 times, 2 ch, sl st in 1st PC. Fasten off. Join B in next 2 ch sp.

Round 3: 3 ch, 1 dc, 2 ch, 2 dc in first ch sp, [3 dc in each of next 2 ch sps, 2 dc, 2 ch, 2 dc in foll ch sp] 3 times, 3 dc in each of next 2 ch sps, sl st in 3rd ch. Fasten off. Join C to a corner 2 ch sp.

Round 4: 3 ch, 1 dc, 2 ch, 2 dc in first ch sp, * [3 dc between next dc group] 3 times, 2 dc, 2 ch, 2 dc in next ch sp, rep from * two more times [3 dc between next dc group] 3 times, sl st in 3rd ch. Fasten off.

HALF FLOWER MOTIF

Using B, make 6 ch, sl st in 1st ch to form a ring.

Row 1 (RS): 1 ch, 6 sc in ring. Fasten off. Join B to 1st sc.

Row 2: 4 ch, 1 PC in 1st sc, [2 ch, 1 PC in next sc] 5 times, 1 ch, 1 dc in last sc. Fasten off. Join C to 4 ch sp.

Row 3: 5 ch, 2 dc in same ch sp, [3 dc in next ch sp] twice, 2 dc, 2 ch, 2 dc in foll ch sp, [3 dc in next ch sp] twice, 2 dc, 2 ch, 1 dc in last ch sp. Fasten off. Join A in 5 ch sp.

Row 4: 5 ch, 2 dc in 5 ch sp, [3 dc between next dc group] 3 times, 2 dc, 2 ch, 2 dc in 2 ch sp, [3 dc between next dc group] 3 times, 2 dc, 2 ch, 1 dc in last ch sp. Fasten off.

SQUARE MOTIF

Using A, make 8 ch, sl st in 1st ch to form a ring.

Round 1 (RS): 1 ch, 12 sc in ring, sl st in 1st sc.

Round 2: 3 ch, 1 dc, 2 ch, 2 dc in 1st dc, 1 ch, skip 2 dc, [2 dc, 2 ch, 2 dc in next sc, 1 ch, skip 2 sc] 3 times, sl st in 3rd ch. Fasten off. Join B to a corner 2 ch sp.

Round 3: 3 ch, 1 dc, 2 ch, 2 dc in 1st 2 ch sp, [1 Fpdc in next dc, 1 dc in foll dc, 1 dc in ch sp, 1 dc in next dc, 1 Fpdc in foll dc, 2 dc, 2 ch, 2 dc in next 2 ch sp] 3 times, 1 Fpdc in next dc, 1 dc in foll dc, 1 dc in ch sp, 1 dc in next dc, 1 Fpdc in foll dc, sl st in 3rd ch. Fasten off.

Join C to a corner 2 ch sp.

Round 4: 3 ch, 1 dc, 2 ch, 2 dc in 1st 2 ch sp, * [1 Fpdc in next st, 1 dc in foll st] 4 times, 1 Fpdc in next st, 2 dc, 2 ch, 2 dc in 2 ch sp, rep from * 2 more times, [1 Fpdc in next st, 1 dc in foll st] 4 times, 1 Fpdc in next st, sl st in 3rd ch. Fasten off.

HALF SQUARE MOTIF

Using B, make 6 ch, sl st in 1st ch to form a ring.

Row 1 (RS): 1 ch, 7 sc in ring. Fasten off. Join B to 1st sc.

Row 2: 5 ch, 2 dc in 1st sc, 1 ch, skip 2 sc, 2 dc, 2 ch, 2 dc in next sc, 1 ch, skip 2 sc, 2 dc, 2 ch, 1 dc in last sc. Fasten off. Join C to 5 ch sp.

Row 3: 5 ch, 2 dc in 5 ch sp, * 1 Fpdc in next dc, 1 dc in foll dc, 1 dc in ch sp, 1 dc in next dc, 1 Fpdc in foll dc *, 2 dc, 2 ch, 2 dc in 2 ch sp, rep from * to *, 2 dc, 2 ch, 1 dc in last ch sp. Fasten off. Join A in 5 ch sp.

Row 4: 5 ch, 2 dc in 5 ch sp, * [1 Fpdc in next st, 1 dc in foll st] 4 times, 1 Fpdc in next st *, 2 dc, 2 ch, 2 dc in 2 ch sp, rep from * to *, 2 dc, 2 ch, 1 dc in last 2 ch sp. Fasten off.

SIDE PANELS

Using B, make 27 (35:43) ch.

Row 1 (RS): 1 dc in 4th ch from hook, 1 dc in each dc to end. [25 (33:41) sts.]

Row 2: 3 ch, skip 1st dc, 1 dc in each dc to last st, 1 dc in 3rd ch.

Row 2 forms double crochet. Cont in dc, work 2 more rows. Place a marker at each side of center 5 dc.

Dec row (RS): 3 ch, skip 1st dc, 1 dc in each dc to 2 dc from 1st marker, 2dctog, slip marker, 1 dc in each of next 5 dc, slip *length*

marker, 2dctog, 1 dc in each st to end.
[23 (31:39) sts.] Decrease in this way at
each side of center 5 dc on next 3 RS rows.
[17 (25:33) sts.] Work 3 rows.

Inc row (RS): 3 ch, skip 1st dc, 1 dc in each
dc to 1 dc from 1st marker, 2 dc in next dc,
slip marker, 1 dc in each of next 5 dc, slip
marker, 2 dc in next dc, 1 dc in each st to
end. [19 (27:35) sts.] Cont in dc, inc in this
way at each side of center 5 dc on 4 foll 4th
rows. [27 (35:43) sts.] Patt 5 rows.

Shape armholes

Row 1: 3 ch, skip 1st dc, 1 dc in each of
next 3 dc, 2dctog, 1 dc in next dc, turn and
complete first side on these 6 sts.
Row 2: 3 ch, 2dctog, 1 dc in each of next
3 sts. [5 sts.]
Row 3: 3 ch, skip 1st dc, 1 dc in next dc,
2dctog, 1 dc in 3rd ch. [4 sts.]
Row 4: 3 ch, skip 1st dc, 2dctog, 1 dc in
3rd ch. [3 sts.] Fasten off. Skip center
13 (21:29) dc join yarn in next dc and work
second side to match.

FINISHING

To join two motifs: Using A, join yarn in
corner 2 ch sp of a motif. With WS together
and taking hook through one st from each
motif each time, work 1 sc in corner sps,
1 sc in each st along edge, 1 sc in corner
sps. Fasten off.

Alternating flower and square motifs and
placing different colorway motifs at random,
join squares to make 6 strips of 8 motifs and
2 strips of 5 motifs. With diagonal edge
toward neck edge, join one half square at
top of each of the 5-motif strips. Working sc
in same way as before along all squares, join
four 8-square strips to form back and one
8-square strip and one 5½-square strip for
each front.

With shaped points at underarm ending
level with the center of the 6th square,
using A and sc, join side panels to front and
back edges. Using A, backstitch over the
line of sc to make it lie flat.

Armhole edgings: With RS facing, join A to
center st at underarm and work 1 round sc
around armhole, sl st in 1st sc. Fasten off.
With WS facing, join C and work 3 rounds
sc. Fasten off.

Front, neck and lower edging: With RS
facing, join A to left back seam, work
1 round sc all around edge, sl st in 1st sc.
Fasten off. With WS facing, join C, work
2 rounds sc, working extra sts and skipping
sts as necessary to keep edging flat.

Buttonhole round: Work in sc until even
with join between half motif and top square
of right front, [3 ch, skip 3 sc, 1 sc in each
of next 11 sc] twice, 3 ch, skip 3 sc, cont in
sc to end. Working 3 sc in each 3 ch sp, work
1 more round sc. Fasten off. Sew on buttons.

Worked primarily in single crochet, this waist-length jacket is very simple to make. The exquisitely shaded colors in the pure wool adds textural interest to an otherwise simple stitch pattern.

ZIP-UP JACKET

HELPFUL HINTS

- Check the front length before buying the zipper. If the zipper is too long, fold the top ends under and secure, then hide the ends inside the collar.

MEASUREMENTS

To fit bust

32	34	36	38	40	42	in
81	86	91	97	102	107	cm

Actual width

36½	38	40	41¾	43½	45¼	in
92.5	97	101.5	106	110.5	115	in

Actual length

19	19½	20	20½	21¼	21½	in
48.5	50	51	52	54	54.5	cm

Actual sleeve

18	18½	18½	18½	19	19	in
46	47	47	47	48	48	cm

In the instructions, figures are given for the smallest size first; larger sizes follow in parentheses. Where only one set of figures is given this applies to all sizes.

MATERIALS

- 11 (12:13:14:15:16) × 50 g balls of Noro Kureyon 139
- H/8 (5.00 mm) crochet hook
- 20 (20:22:22:22:22) in (50 (50:55:55:55:55) cm) separating zipper

GAUGE

15 sts and 18 rows to 4 in (10 cm) measured over single crochet using H/8 (5.00 mm) hook. Change hook size if necessary to obtain this gauge.

ABBREVIATIONS

2sctog – leaving loop on hook each time, sl st in each of next 2 sts, yo and pull though 3 loops on hook
See also page 9.

JACKET

The body of the jacket is worked in one piece from front to front so the rows run the length of the garment and the shaded yarn makes vertical stripes.

Left front

Make 61 (61:63:64:67:68) ch.
Row 1: 1 sc in 2nd ch from hook, 1 sc in each ch to end. [60 (60:62:63:66:67) sts.]
Row 2 (RS): 1 ch, 1 sc in each sc to end.
2nd row forms single crochet.
Cont in sc, work 9 (11:11:11:11:13) more rows.

Shape neck

Inc row (RS): 1 ch, 1 sc in each sc to last sc, 2 sc in last sc.
Cont in sc, inc in this way at end of next

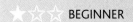 *Long glass-headed quilting pins are ideal for pinning the zipper in place.*

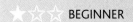 *Don't join in new yarn at the lower edge of the back and fronts. It's easier to hide the ends if you start a new ball at the top edge or during a row.*

3 RS rows. [64 (64:66:67:70:71) sts.] At end of last row, make 10 (12:12:12:12:12) ch, turn.

Shape shoulder
Next row (WS): 1 sc in 2nd ch from hook, 1 sc in each sc to end.
[73 (75:77:78:81:82) sts.] Cont in sc, work 12 (12:14:16:18:18) rows.

Shape side and left armhole
** Row 1 (RS): 1 ch, 1 sc in each of next 10 sc, sl st in each of next 15 sc, 1 sc in each sc to end.
Row 2: 1 ch, 1 sc in each of next 48 (50:52:53:56:57) sc, 1 sc in each of next 15 sl st, 1 sc in each of next 10 sc.
Row 3: 1 ch, 1 sc in each of next 10 sc, sl st in each of next 15 sc, 1 sc in each of next 26 (26:27:27:28:28) sc, turn.
Rows 4, 6 and 8: 1 ch, skip 1st sc, 1 sc in each sc to sl st, 1 sc in each sl st, 1 sc in each sc to end.
Row 5: 1 ch, 1 sc in each of next 10 sc, sl st in each of next 15 sc, 1 sc in each of next 24 (24:25:25:26:26) sc, turn.
Row 7: 1 ch, 1 sc in each of next 10 sc, sl st in each of next 15 sc, 1 sc in each of next 22 (22:23:23:24:24) sc, turn.
Row 9: 1 ch, 1 sc in each of next 10 sc, sl st in each of next 15 sc, 1 sc in each of next 20 (20:21:21:22:22) sc, turn.

[45 (45:46:46:47:47) sts.]
Shaping by working sl st in same way as before, work 4 rows.
Rows 14, 16 and 18: 1 ch, 2 sc in 1st sc, 1 sc in each st to end.
Rows 15, 17 and 19: 1 ch, 1 sc in each of next 10 sc, sl st in each of next 15 sc, 1 sc in each sc to last sc, 2 sc in last sc.
[51 (51:52:52:53:53) sts.] At end of last row, make 23 (25:26:27:29:30) ch, turn.

Shape back
Row 1 (WS): 1 sc in 2nd ch from hook, 1 sc in each st to end.
Row 2: 1 ch, 1 sc in each of next 10 sc, sl st in each of next 15 sc, 1 sc in each sc to end.
[73 (75:77:78:81:82) sts **.]
Cont in sc, work 63 (67:71:75:79:83) rows.

Shape side and right armhole
Work as given for shape side and left armhole from ** to **.

Shape shoulder
Cont in sc, work 13 (13:15:17:19:19) rows.

Shape neck
Row 1 (RS): 1 ch, 1 sc in each sc to last 9 (11:11:11:11:11) sc, turn.
[64 (64:66:67:70:71) sts.]
Dec row (WS): 1 ch, skip 1 st sc, 1 sc in each sc to end.

Cont in sc, dec in this way at beg of next 3 WS rows. [60 (60:62:63:66:67) sts.]
Cont in sc, work 10 (12:12:12:12:14) rows. Fasten off.

SLEEVES (MAKE 2)

Make 34 (34:36:36:38:38) ch.
Row 1 (WS): 1 sc in 2nd ch from hook, 1 sc in each ch to end. [33 (33:35:35:37:37) sts.]
Row 2 (RS): 1 ch, 1 sc in each sc to end.
Row 2 forms single crochet.
Work 15 (13:13:13:9:3) more rows sc.
Inc row (RS): 1 ch, 1 sc in 1st sc, 2 sc in next sc, 1 sc in each sc to last 2 sc, 2 sc in next sc, 1 sc in last sc.
[35 (35:37:37:39:39) sts.]
Cont in sc, inc in this way at each end of 7 (8:10:11:12:13) foll 8th (8th:6th:6th: 6th:6th) rows. [49 (51:57:59:63:65) sts.]
Work 9 (5:9:3:3:3) rows.

Shape top

Next row (RS): Sl st in each of first 3 sc, 1 ch, 1 sc in each sc to last 3 sc, turn.
[43 (45:51:53:57:59) sts.]
Dec row: 1 ch, skip 1st sc, 1 sc in each sc to last 2 sc, 2sctog.
[41 (43:49:51:55:57) sts.]
Cont in sc, dec in this way at each end of next 13 (14:16:17:19:20) rows.
[15 (15:17:17:17:17) sts.] Fasten off.

COLLAR

Matching sts, join shoulders.
Row 1 (RS): Join yarn 2 rows in from right front edge, work 23 (24:24:24:24:25) sl st up right front neck, 24 (26:26:26:26:28) sl st across back neck and 23 (24:24:24:24:25) sl st down left front neck to last 2 rows.
[70 (74:74:74:74:78) sts.]
Row 2: 1 ch, 1 sc in each sl st to end.
Row 3: 1 ch, 1 sc in each dc to end.
Row 3 forms single crochet. Work 1 more row sc.
Dec row (RS): 1 ch, 1 sc in each of first 2 sc, [2sctog, 1 sc in each of next 2 sc] to end. [53 (56:56:56:56:59) sts.]
Cont in sc until collar measures 6 in (15 cm), ending with a WS row.
Inc row (RS): 1 ch, 1 sc in each of first 2 sc, [2 sc in next sc, 1 sc in each of next 2 sc] to end. [70 (74:74:74:74:78) sts.]
Work 2 rows sc. Fasten off.
Edgings: With RS facing, join yarn and work 28 sl st across row-ends of collar, turn and work 1 ch, 1 sc in each sl st to end. Fasten off. Work other side to match.

FINISHING

Press according to ball band. Mark center of collar at each front edge. Set in zipper, ending at markers. Fold collar in half to WS, sew edgings to zipper, then slipstitch last row of collar to neck edge. Join sleeve

SETTING A ZIPPER IN A CROCHET GARMENT

Make sure the zipper opens and closes properly, then lay it on a flat surface with the RS of the zip and jacket facing. Slip the zipper flange under the front edges. Setting the pins at right angles to the edge, pin the zipper in place. Check that the stitches along each edge of the jacket line up, and that the crochet fabric and zipper are lying flat. Baste the zipper in place. Remove the pins, open the zipper and turn the jacket inside out. Slipstitch the edge of the zipper flange in place. Follow the same line of crochet stitches up the front so the edges are straight. Zip up the zipper again to check that both sides match. Unzip the zipper and with RS facing, backstitch through the crochet fabric and zipper as near to the teeth as possible, removing the basting thread as you sew. Keep the needle vertical and work one stitch at a time, stitching in a stabbing motion. Don't scoop through the layers or they may slip and become bumpy.

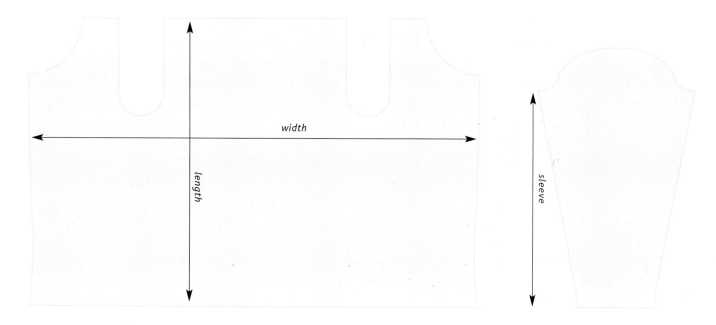

seams. Match sleeve seam to center of underarm and shoulder seam to center top of sleeve, then, easing to fit, set in sleeves.

VARIATION

ZIP-UP VEST

To make a zip-up vest, simply omit the sleeves and neaten the armhole edges with a few rounds of sc.

You will need approximately 7 (8:8:9:10:11) × 50 g balls of Noro Kureyon.

Made using just one skein of yarn, this wild and woolly scarf does double duty in keeping you both warm and fashionable during the cold winter months.

LOOPY STITCH BOA

⭐☆☆ BEGINNER

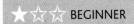 *Make the foundation chain loosely. If necessary, use a hook that is a size larger than stated in the directions.*

HELPFUL HINTS

- Loop stitch is really just a single crochet with the middle strand of yarn elongated. It is worked on wrong side rows so that the loops show on the right side.

MEASUREMENTS

1¾ × 53 in
4.5 × 134 cm

MATERIALS

- 1 × 100 g hank of Debbie Bliss Maya in Red 10
- K/10½ (6.50 mm) crochet hook

GAUGE

8½ sts to 4 in (10 cm), 6 rows measure 1¾ in (4.5 cm) over loop stitch patt using K/10½ (6.50 mm) hook. Change hook size if necessary to obtain this gauge.

ABBREVIATIONS

Lp1 (loop one) – insert hook, extend middle finger to form a loop, catch back and front strands of the loop of yarn with hook and pull through to make 3 loops on hook, take hook to left of long loop on finger, yarn over hook and pull through to secure the 3 loops, remove finger
See also page 9.

BOA

Make 115 ch.
Row 1: Lp1 in 2nd ch from hook, work Lp1 in each ch to end. [114 sts.]
Row 2 (WS): 1 ch, work Lp1 in each st to end.
Row 3: 1 ch, work 1 sc in each st to end.
Rows 2 and 3 form loop st patt.
Patt 3 more rows. Fasten off.
Steam lightly on WS. Weave in ends.

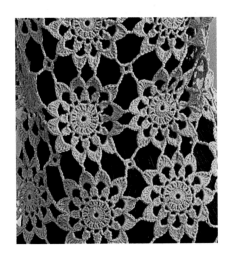

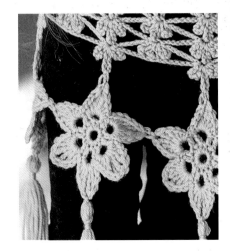

WEEKEND

From town chic to country casual, you can relax and unwind in style with these fabulous fashions. If you want something you can crochet and wear in the same weekend, choose an attractive, fast-working project like the chunky beret or the flower-and-mesh scarf. If you're out and about, wrap up in the figure-skimming, shaded coat in a lightweight, textured yarn. Brighten up a dull day or a plain outfit with the tassel-edged wrap in a stunning color. And if your weekend starts on a Friday night, make the flower motif long cardigan for the ultimate transition from day-to-evening.

CHUNKY BLUE BERET

BEGINNER

Check that your foundation chain will fit around your head, if it is too tight, redo it working more loosely.

Do not count the 1 ch at the beginning of single crochet rounds as a stitch, simply sl st in the first sc, then on the next round, work the first sc in the same sc as the sl st of the previous round.

Count the 3 ch at the beginning of double crochet rounds as a stitch.

Work the 3rd ch at the beginning of double crochet rounds loosely. This will make it easier to insert the hook under both loops of the 3rd ch to work the sl st at the end to join the round.

HELPFUL HINTS

- The beret is worked in the round so there is no sewing up, just darn in the ends and it's ready to wear.

MEASUREMENTS

Finished circumference
23 in
58 cm

MATERIALS

- 2 × 100 g balls of Sirdar Bigga in Delta Blue 688
- N/15 (10.00 mm) crochet hook

GAUGE

5½ sts and 3 rows to 4 in (10 cm) measured over treble crochet using N/15 (10.00 mm) hook. Change hook size if necessary to obtain this gauge.

ABBREVIATIONS

2sctog – insert hook in next st, yo and pull loop through, insert hook in foll st, yo and pull loop through, yo and pull through 3 loops on hook
2dctog – leaving last loop of each st on hook, work 1 dc in each of next 2 sts, yo and pull through 3 loops on hook
See also page 9.

BERET

Leaving a 6-in (15-cm) end, make 33 ch.
Round 1: 1 sc in 2nd ch from hook, 1 sc in each ch to end, turn and sl st in 1st st to join in a round. [32 sts.]
Rounds 2 and 3 (RS): 1 ch, 1 sc in each sc to end, sl st in 1st sc.
Round 4: 3 ch, 1 dc in same sc as sl st, 1 dc in each of next 2 sc, [2 dc in each of next 2 sc, 1 dc in each of foll 2 sc] 7 times, 2 dc in last sc, sl st in 3rd ch. [48 sts.]
Round 5: 3 ch, 1 dc in each dc to end, sl st in 3rd ch.
Round 6: 2 ch, 1 dc in each of next 3 dc, * [2dctog] twice, 1 dc in each of next 2 dc, rep from * 6 more times, 2dctog, sl st in 1st dc. [32 sts.]
Round 7: 2 ch, 1 dc in next dc, [2dctog] 15 times, sl st in 1st dc. [16 sts.]
Round 8: 2 ch, 1 dc in next dc, [2dctog] 7 times, sl st in 1st dc. [8 sts.]
Round 9: [2sctog] 4 times, sl st in 1st st. [4 sts.]
Leaving a 6-in (15-cm) end, fasten off.

FINISHING

Thread end through front loop of each st of Round 9, draw up and secure. Weave in ends at beginning of 2nd ball of yarn. Join 1st and last sts of Round 1 while weaving end at beginning of Round 1.

This beautiful scarf in hot pink yarn is incredibly quick to finish – just eleven rows to crochet and you're ready to wrap it around your neck and shoulders, a fashionable accent to any outfit.

FLOWER-AND-MESH PATTERNED SCARF

MEASUREMENTS
Actual width
9 in
23 cm
Actual length (including tassels)
102 in
260 cm

MATERIALS
- 4 × 100 g balls of Rowan Big Wool in Whoosh 14
- N/15 (10.00 mm) crochet hook

GAUGE
16 sts (two repeats) measure 12 in (30 cm). 5 rows to 4 in (10 cm) measured over pattern using N/15 (10.00 mm) hook. Change hook size if necessary to obtain this gauge.

ABBREVIATIONS
2dccl – leaving last loop of each st on hook, work 2 dc in stitch indicated, yo and pull through 3 loops on hook
See also page 9.

SCARF
Make a slip knot and work 2 ch, 1 sc in 2nd ch from hook, * inserting hook under two strands at bottom left of previous sc, work 1 sc in previous sc, rep from * until there are 117 sts.

Row 1 (WS): 1 ch, 1 sc in each sc to end.
Row 2: 1 ch, 1 sc in 1st sc, 3 ch, 2 dccl in sc at beg, skip 3 sc, 2 dccl in next sc, 3 ch, sl st in same sc, [6 ch, skip 3 sc, sl st in next sc, 3 ch, 2 dccl in same sc, skip 3 sc, 2 dccl in next sc, 3 ch, sl st in same sc] 14 times.
Row 3: 5 ch, 2 dccl in top of first 2 dccl, 3 ch, sl st in same 2 dccl, 3 ch, 2 dccl in same 2 dccl, [3 ch, 1 sc in 6 ch sp, 3 ch, 2 dccl in top of next 2 dccl, 3 ch, sl st in same 2 dccl, 3 ch, 2 dccl in same 2 dccl] 14 times, 1 dtr in last sc.
Row 4: 1 ch, 1 sc in dtr, [3 ch, 1 sc in top of next 2 dccl] to end.
Row 5: 1 ch, 1 sc in 1st sc, [3 sc in 3 ch sp, 1 sc in next sc] to end.
Row 6: 1 ch, 1 sc in each sc to end.
Row 7: As row 2.
Row 8: As row 3.
Row 9: As row 4.
Row 10: As row 5.
Row 11: As row 6.
Fasten off.

FINISHING
Join yarn and work 16 sc across one short edge. Work 2 more rows sc. Fasten off. Finish the other short edge in the same way. Using ten 16½ in (42 cm) lengths of yarn for each tassel, make 10 tassels. Sew 5 tassels on each short edge. Press according to instructions on ball band. Trim tassels.

★☆☆ BEGINNER

Starting with a sc chain gives a more flexible edge. A sc chain is also easier to count than basic chain.

Work the 3 ch on the 4th row loosely so the row doesn't pull in.

When working into top of 2 dccl, lift the loose strand below with the hook and work into this strand and the front loop of the stitch.

⚬	ch
	sl st
+	sc
⊕	scch
	2dccl
	dtr

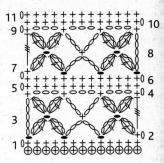

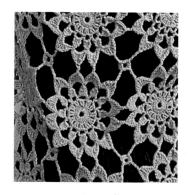

LACY MOTIFS LONG CARDIGAN

Big flower wheel motifs in fingering weight cotton are joined together in rows to make this dramatically long cardigan. A subtle realignment of the motifs at the underarms gives a slender line to the sleeve tops.

★★★ ADVANCED

 The second size has the same number of motifs joined in the same way as the first size but the motifs are worked on a larger hook to make them bigger. The gauge can vary a lot in crochet and as the size of the cardigan depends on the size of each flower motif, do check your gauge carefully. If your motif is too big, try again using a smaller hook, if it is too small, try again using a larger hook.

This motif uses several different height stitches to make the outer petals. Here's a reminder of how many times to take the yarn over the hook at the start of each stitch: sc = zero times, hdc = once but pull through all first time; dc = once; tr = twice, dtr = 3 times.

HELPFUL HINTS

- Fingering weight cotton can be slippery. If you need to increase the gauge on the supply yarn, take it around the little finger in the usual way, then over and around the middle finger as well.
- To make a neat center for the flower motif, wind the yarn around index finger of left hand, insert hook, yo and pull through. Work over end as well as into ring, then before joining Round 1 pull the end to tighten the ring. Weave in end securely before trimming it off.
- Instructions are given for joining lines of flower motifs, then working a line of filler motifs. However, you can work fillers each time there's a space.

MEASUREMENTS
To fit bust

32–36	38–42	in
81–91	97–107	cm

Actual width

36	42½	in
92	108	cm

Actual length

31½	37	in
80.5	94.5	cm

Actual sleeve

18	21¼	in
46	54	cm

In the instructions, figures are given for the smaller size first; larger size follows in parentheses. Where only one set of figures is given this applies to both sizes.

MATERIALS

- 5 (6) × 100 g balls of Patons 100% Cotton 4-ply in Ocean 01711
- B/1 (D/3) (2.25 (3.25) mm) crochet hook

GAUGE
One flower motif measures 4½ (5¼) in (11.5 (13.5) cm) across when pressed, using B/1 (D/3) (2.25 (3.25) mm) hook. Change hook size if necessary to obtain this gauges.

ABBREVIATIONS
4trcl – leaving last loop of each st on hook, work 4tr, yo and pull through all 5 loops on hook
See also page 9.

CARDIGAN

BACK AND FRONTS

1st line of flower motifs

1st motif: Wind yarn around finger to form a ring.

Round 1 (RS): 3 ch, work 23 dc in ring, pull end to tighten ring, sl st in 3rd ch. [24 sts.]

Round 2: 3 ch, 1 dc in same place as sl st, 1 ch, skip 1 dc, [2 dc in next dc, 1 ch, skip 1 dc] 11 times, 1 ch, sl st in 3rd ch.

Round 3: Sl st in 1st dc, 1 sc in 1st 1 ch sp, 5 ch, [1 sc in next 1 ch sp, 5 ch] 11 times, sl st in 1st sc.

Round 4: Sl st in each of first 3 ch, 4 ch, leaving last loop of each st on hook, work 3 tr in ch sp, yo and pull through all 4 loops on hook to make first 4trcl, [7 ch, 4trcl in next 5 ch sp] 11 times, 7 ch, sl st in 1st trcl.

Round 5: [1 sc, 1 hdc, 1 dc, 2 tr, 2 ch, 2 tr, 1 dc, 1 hdc, 1 sc in next 7 ch sp] 12 times, sl st in 1st sc. Fasten off.

2nd and following motifs

Work as given for 1st motif until Round 4 has been completed.

Round 5: [1 sc, 1 hdc, 1 dc, 2 tr, 2 ch, 2 tr, 1 dc, 1 hdc, 1 sc in next 7 ch sp] 10 times, in next 7 ch sp, work *1 sc, 1 hdc, 1 dc, 2 tr, 1 ch, with WS together, join with a dc in a 2 ch sp of 1st motif, 2 tr, 1 dc, 1 hdc, 1 sc, rep from * in next 7 ch sp joining to next 2 ch sp of 1st motif, sl st in 1st sc. Fasten off.

Make 6 more motifs, joining motifs in the same way. Lay the line of motifs flat. The 1st and 2nd motifs on the left are the left front, the next 4 motifs are the back, and the last 2 motifs are the right front.

2nd line of flower motifs

1st motif: Work as given for 1st motif of first line of flower motifs until Round 4 has been completed. Work Round 5 until 10 petals have been completed, then join 11th and 12th petals to top two petals of 1st motif of left front.

2nd motif: Work as 1st motif until 7 petals have been completed. Join 8th and 9th petals to 1st motif of 2nd line, work one petal, join 11th and 12th petals to top two petals of 2nd motif of 1st line, so leaving 4 petals free at center of join.

Make 6 more motifs joining in same way as 2nd motif.

Filler motif: Each filler motif is worked in the four petals free between lines of flower motifs. Make 8 ch, sl st in 1st ch to form a ring.

Round 1: With WS together each time, work 1 dtr in 2 ch sp of 1st motif, 3 sc in ring, [1 dtr in 2 ch sp of next motif, 3 sc in ring] 3 times, sl st in 1st dtr.

Fasten off. Work a filler motif in each of the remaining 6 spaces.

3rd 4th and 5th lines of flower motifs:

Work and join motifs in the same way as 2nd line of flower motifs, working filler motifs between each line of motifs.

Divide for armhole

6th line of flower motifs: Work and join 1st and 2nd motifs. Omitting join between 2nd

Keep a slim blunt-pointed needle handy and weave in ends as you work, then all you need to do is press your cardigan before you wear it.

Spray lightly with starch before pressing.

and 3rd motifs for left armhole, join 3rd motif to 3rd motif of 5th line of flower motifs, then join 4th, 5th and 6th motifs in the usual way. Omitting join between 6th and 7th motifs for right armhole, join 7th motif to 7th motif of 5th line of flower motifs, then join 8th motif in the usual way. Work filler motifs between 5th and 6th lines of motifs.

Shape neck

One motif is omitted at each end of 7th line and front and back motifs are joined at shoulders

7th line of motifs

1st motif: Join to 2nd motif of 6th line of flower motifs.
2nd motif: Work until 4 petals of Round 5 have been completed. Join 5th and 6th petals to top two petals of 1st motif of 7th line, work 4 petals, join 11th and 12th petals to top two petals of 3rd motif of 6th line of flower motifs.
3rd, 4th and 5th motifs: Join in the usual way.
6th motif: Work until 4 petals of Round 5 have been completed. Join 5th and 6th petals to top two petals of 5th motif of 7th line, work 4 petals, join 11th and 12th petals to top two petals of 7th motif of 6th line of flower motifs. Work a filler motif in each of the 3 spaces between the four motifs of the back, then work a triangle filler motif between three adjacent petals at each side of front neck.

Triangle filler motif

Make 8 ch, sl st in 1st ch to form a ring.
Round 1: With WS together each time, work 1 dtr in 2 ch sp of 1st motif, 3 sc in ring, [1 dtr in 2 ch sp of next motif, 3 sc in ring] twice, sl st in 1st dtr.

Join petals at neck edge

Leave two petals following triangle filler at neck edge of 6th motif of 7th line and join yarn in last petal. Work 10 ch, 1 sc in next petal of 5th motif of 7th line, 10 ch, sl st in next petal of 4th motif of 7th line. Fasten off. Leave next 2 petals of 4th motif of 7th line and join yarn in last petal. Work 10 ch, sl st in next petal of 3rd motif of 7th line. Fasten off. Leave next 2 petals of 3rd motif of 7th line and join yarn in last petal. 10 ch, 1 sc in next petal of 2nd motif of 7th line, 10 ch, sl st in next petal of 1st motif of 7th line. Fasten off.

LEFT SLEEVE

1st line of motifs

The 1st motif is placed at the underarm and joins four petals consecutively at the underarm.
1st motif: Work until 8 petals of Round 5 have been completed. Skip one petal of 2nd motif of 6th line, join 9th and 10th petals to remaining 2 petals of 2nd motif of 6th line, then join 11th and 12th petals to next 2 petals of 3rd motif of 6th line.

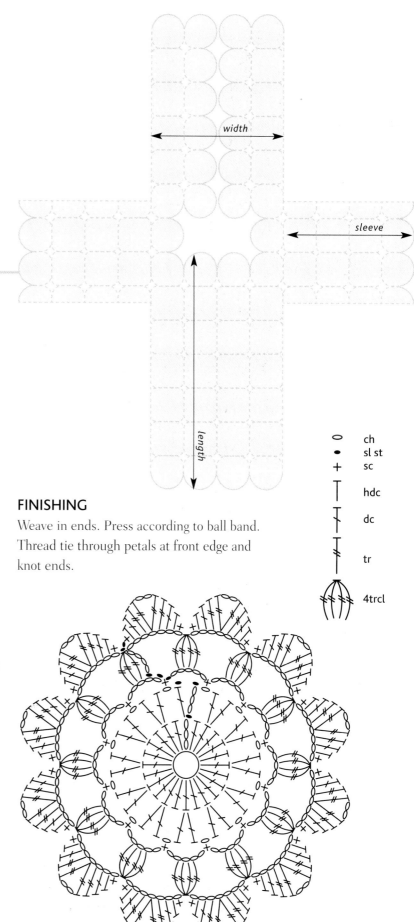

2nd motif: Work until 7 petals of Round 5 have been completed. Join 8th and 9th petals to center two petals of 1st motif of 7th line, work one petal, join 11th and 12th petals to next 2 petals of 1st sleeve motif.

3rd motif: Work until 4 petals of Round 5 have been completed, skip 4 petals and join 5th and 6th petals in last 2 petals of 1st sleeve motif, work one petal, skip one petal and join 8th and 9th petals in next 2 petals of 2nd motif of 7th line, work one petal, skip one petal and join 11th and 12th petals in next 2 petals of 2nd motif of 1st line of sleeve. Work a filler motif in the 4-petal space on the shoulder and a triangle filler motif in each 3-petal space at each side.

2nd, 3rd and 4th lines of motifs

Join 3 motifs in a round for each line and work filler motifs between.

RIGHT SLEEVE

Work as left sleeve but joining 1st motif into 6th and 7th motifs of 6th line at underarm, 2nd motif into 5th motif of 7th line and 3rd motif into 6th motif of 7th line of motifs.

TIE

Make 2 ch, 1 sc in 2nd ch from hook, working under 2 strands at side of sc each time, * work 1 sc in previous dc, repeat from * until tie measures 21½ in (55 cm). Fasten off.

FINISHING

Weave in ends. Press according to ball band. Thread tie through petals at front edge and knot ends.

○	ch
•	sl st
+	sc
T	hdc
⊤	dc
⊤	tr
⊕	4trcl

Worked primarily in double crochet, this wrap-style coat is designed to maximize the variations of the lightweight bouclé yarn in shades of pink and purple.

SHADED BLANKET COAT

 *Although this is a textured yarn, it's easy to crochet with because the bouclé loops are too small and closely spaced to catch on the hook.*

The back and fronts of the coat are worked in one piece to the armholes so the shading in the yarn flows around the body. The shading on the sleeves is wider than the color stripes on the body because the rows are shorter.

Use left over yarn to make a scarf. Simply make picots until the scarf is the width you want, then work in double crochet until the scarf is the length you want. Finish off the edges with picots.

HELPFUL HINTS

- The picot edging is not just decorative. In this yarn it is easier to work into and between picots than to find the loops of a foundation chain.
- When working the two rows to divide the back and fronts and shape the underarms, it's important to break and rejoin the yarn for each section to keep the continuity of the color shading.

MEASUREMENTS

To fit bust

32–34	36–38	40–42	44–46	in
81–86	91–97	102–107	112–117	cm

Actual width

35	39¼	43½	47¾	in
89	100	110.5	121.5	cm

Actual length

31½	32	32¾	33½	in
80	81.5	83	85	cm

Actual sleeve seam

19 in
48 cm

In the instructions, figures are given for the smallest size first; larger sizes follow in parentheses. Where only one set of figures is given this applies to all sizes.

MATERIALS

- 2 × 400 g balls of Sirdar Yo-Yo in Damson Mist 14
- H/8 (5.00 mm) crochet hook

GAUGE

11 sts and 6 rows to 4 in (10 cm) measured over double crochet stitch using H/8 (5.00 mm) hook. Change hook size if necessary to obtain this gauge.

ABBREVIATIONS

2dctog – leaving last loop of each st on hook, work a double crochet in each of next 2 sts, yo and pull through 3 loops on hook
See also page 9.

COAT

BACK AND FRONTS

Row 1: 3 ch, 1 sc in 1st ch, [4 ch, 1 sc in 3rd ch] 72 (78:84:90) times.
Row 2 (WS): 1 sc in 1st picot, 2 ch, [1 dc between picots, 1 dc in next picot] 72 (78:84:90) times. [145 (157:169:181) sts.]
Row 3: 1 sc in 1st dc, 2 ch, 1 dc in each dc to last st, 1 dc in 2nd ch.
Row 3 forms double crochet. Cont in dc, work 17 more rows.
Dec row 1 (RS): 1 sc in 1st dc, 2 ch, 1 dc in each of next 33 (36:39:42) dc, [2trtog] 4 times, 1 dc in each of next 61 (67:73:79) dc,

[2dctog] 4 times, 1 dc in each of next 33 (36:39:42) dc, 1 dc in 2nd ch. [137 (149:161: 173) sts.] Cont in dc, work 3 rows.

Dec row 2: 1 sc in 1st dc, 2 ch, 1 dc in each of next 31 (34:37:40) dc, [2dctog] 4 times, 1 dc in each of next 57 (63:69:75) dc, [2trtog] 4 times, 1 dc in each of next 31 (34:37:40) dc, 1 dc in 2nd ch. [129 (141:153:165) sts.] Cont in dc, work 3 rows.

Dec row 3: 1 sc in 1st dc, 2 ch, 1 dc in each of next 29 (32:35:38) dc, [2dctog] 4 times, 1 dc in each of next 53 (59:65:71) dc, [2dctog] 4 times, 1 dc in each of next 29 (32:35:38) dc, 1 dc in 2nd ch. [121 (133:145:157) sts.] Cont in dc, work 3 rows.

Dec row 4: 1 sc in 1st dc, 2 ch, 1 dc in each of next 27 (30:33:36) dc, [2dctog] 4 times, 1 dc in each of next 49 (55:61:67) dc, [2dctog] 4 times, 1 dc in each of next 27 (30:33:36) dc, 1 dc in 2nd ch. [113 (125:137:149) sts.] Cont in dc, work 3 rows.

Dec row 5: 1 sc in 1st dc, 2 ch, 1 dc in each of next 25 (28:31:34) dc, [2dctog] 4 times, 1 dc in each of next 45 (51:57:63) dc, [2dctog] 4 times, 1 dc in each of next 25 (28:31:34) dc, 1 dc in 2nd ch. [105 (117:129:141) sts.] Cont in dc, work one row.

Divide for armholes and shape collar

Row 1 (RS): 1 sc in 1st dc, 2 ch, 1 dc in same dc, 1 dc in each of next 25 (28:31:34) dc, fasten off and break yarn, skip 4 dc, join yarn in next dc, 3 ch, 1 dc in each of next 44 (50:56:62) dc, fasten off and break yarn, skip 4 dc, join yarn in next dc, 3 ch, 1 dc in each of next 24 (27:30:33) dc, 2 dc in 2nd ch. [27 (30:33:36) sts in each front and 45 (51:57:63) sts in back.]

Row 2: 1 sc in 1st dc, 2 ch, 1 dc in same dc, 1 dc in each of next 23 (26:29:32) dc, 2dctog, 1 dc in 3rd ch, fasten off and break yarn, join yarn in 1st dc of back, 3 ch, 2dctog, 1 dc in each of next 39 (45:51:57) dc, 2dctog, 1 dc in 3rd ch, fasten off and break yarn, join yarn in 1st dc of right front, 3 ch, 2dctog, 1 dc in each of next 23 (26:29:32) dc, 2 dc in 2nd ch. [27 (30:33:36) sts in each front and 43 (49:55:61) sts in back.] Do not fasten off, leave back and fronts with yarn attached.

SLEEVES (MAKE 2)

Make 15 (16:17:18) picots as given for back. Work Row 1 as given for back and fronts. [29 (31:33:35) sts.] Cont in dc as given for back, work 6 (6:2:2) rows.

Inc row: 1 sc in 1st dc, 2 ch, 1 dc in same dc, 1 dc in each dc to last st, 2 dc in 2nd ch. [31 (33:35:37) sts.] Cont in dc, inc in this way at each end of 5 (5:6:6) foll 4th rows. [41 (43:47:49) sts.] Work 1 row.

Shape top

Row 1: (RS) Sl st in each of first 4 dc, 3 ch, 1 dc in each of next 34 (36:40:42) dc, turn and

leave 3 sts. [35 (37:41:43) sts.]

Dec row: 1 sc in 1st dc, 2 ch, 2dctog, 1 dc in each of next 29 (31:35:37) dc, 2dctog, 1 dc in 3rd ch. [33 (35:39:41) sts.] Fasten off.

YOKE

Row 1 (RS): Across 27 (30:33:36) sts of right front work 1 sc in 1st dc, 2 ch, 1 dc in same dc, 1 dc in each of next 22 (25:28:31) dc, [2dctog] twice, across 33 (35:39:41) sts of right sleeve work * [2trtog] twice, 1 dc in each of next 25 (27:31:33) dc, [2dctog] twice *, across 43 (49:55:61) sts of back work [2dctog] twice, 1 dc in each of next 35 (41:47:53) dc, [2dctog] twice, rep from * to * across 33 (35:39:41) sts of left sleeve, across 27 (30:33:36) sts of left front work [2dctog] twice, 1 dc in each of next 22 (25:28:31) dc, 2 dc in 2nd ch. [149 (165:185:201) sts.]

Row 2: 1 sc in 1st dc, 2 ch, 1 dc in same dc, 1 dc in each of next 21 (24:27:30) dc, [2dctog] 4 times, 1 dc in each of next 21 (23:27:29) dc, [2dctog] 4 times, 1 dc in each of next 31 (37:43:49) dc, [2dctog] 4 times, 1 dc in each of next 21 (23:27:29) dc, [2dctog] 4 times, 1 dc in each of next 21 (24:27:30) dc, 2 dc in 2nd ch. [135 (151:171:187) sts.]

Row 3: 1 sc in 1st dc, 2 ch, 1 dc in same dc, 1 dc in each of next 20 (23:26:29) dc, [2dctog] 4 times, 1 dc in each of next 17 (19:23:25) dc, [2dctog] 4 times, 1 dc in each of next 27 (33:39:45) dc, [2dctog] 4 times, 1 dc in each of next 17 (19:23:25) dc, [2dctog] 4 times, 1 dc in each of next 20 (23:26:29) dc, 2 dc in 2nd ch. [121 (137:157:173) sts.]

Row 4: 1 dc in 1st dc, 2 ch, 1 dc in same dc, 1 dc in each of next 19 (22:25:28) dc, [2dctog] 4 times, 1 dc in each of next 13 (15:19:21) dc, [2dctog] 4 times, 1 dc in each of next 23 (29:35:41) dc, [2dctog] 4 times, 1 dc in each of next 13 (15:19:21) dc, [2dctog] 4 times, 1 dc in each of next 19 (22:25:28) dc, 2 dc in 2nd ch. [107 (123:143:159) sts.]

Row 5: 1 sc in 1st dc, 2 ch, 1 dc in same dc, 1 dc in each of next 18 (21:24:27) dc, [2dctog] 4 times, 1 dc in each of next 9 (11:15:17) dc, [2dctog] 4 times, 1 dc in each of next 19 (25:31:37) dc, [2dctog] 4 times, 1 dc in each of next 9 (11:15:17) dc, [2dctog] 4 times, 1 dc in each of next 18 (21:24:27) dc, 2 dc in 2nd ch. [93 (109:129:145) sts.]

Row 6: 1 sc in 1st dc, 2 ch, 1 dc in same dc, 1 dc in each of next 17 (20:23:26) dc, [2dctog] 4 times, 1 dc in each of next 5 (7:11:13) dc, [2dctog] 4 times, 1 dc in each of next 15 (21:27:33) dc, [2dctog] 4 times, 1 dc in each of next 5 (7:11:13) dc, [2dctog] 4 times, 1 dc in each of next 17 (20:23:26) dc, 2 dc in 2nd ch. [79 (95:115:131) sts.]

2nd size only

Row 7: 1 sc in 1st dc, 2 ch, 1 dc in same dc, 1 dc in each of next 19 dc, [2dctog] 3 times, 1 dc in each of next 7 dc, [2dctog] 3 times, 1 dc in each of next 17 dc, [2dctog] 3 times, 1 dc

in each of next 7 dc, [2dctog] 3 times, 1 dc in each of next 19 dc, 2 dc in 2nd ch. [85 sts.]

3rd size only

Row 7: 1 sc in 1st dc, 2 ch, 1 dc in same dc, 1 dc in each of next 22 dc, [2dctog] 4 times, 1 dc in each of next 7 dc, [2dctog] 4 times, 1 dc in each of next 22 dc, [2dctog] 4 times, 1 dc in each of next 7 dc, [2dctog] 4 times, 1 dc in each of next 22 dc, 2 dc in 2nd ch. [101 sts.]

Row 8: 1 sc in 1st dc, 2 ch, 1 dc in same dc, 1 dc in each of next 21 dc, [2dctog] 3 times, 1 dc in each of next 7 dc, [2dctog] 3 times, 1 dc in each of next 19 dc, [2dctog] 3 times, 1 dc

in each of next 7 dc, [2dctog] 3 times, 1 dc in each of next 21 dc, 2 dc in 2nd ch. [91 sts.]

4th size only

Row 7: 1 sc in 1st dc, 2 ch, 1 dc in same dc, 1 dc in each of next 25 dc, [2dctog] 4 times, 1 dc in each of next 9 dc, [2dctog] 4 times, 1 dc in each of next 29 dc, [2dctog] 4 times, 1 dc in each of next 9 dc, [2dctog] 4 times, 1 dc in each of next 25 dc, 2 dc in 2nd ch. [117 sts.]

Row 8: 1 sc in 1st dc, 2 ch, 1 dc in same dc, 1 dc in each of next 24 dc, [2dctog] 3 times, 1 dc in each of next 9 dc, [2dctog] 3 times, 1 dc in each of next 25 dc, [2dctog] 3 times, 1 dc in each of next 9 dc, [2dctog] 3 times, 1 dc in each of next 24 dc, 2 dc in 2nd ch. [107 sts.]

Row 9: 1 sc in 1st dc, 2 ch, 1 dc in same dc, 1 dc in each of next 23 dc, [2dctog] 3 times, 1 dc in each of next 7 dc, [2dctog] 3 times, 1 dc in each of next 21 dc, [2dctog] 3 times, 1 dc in each of next 7 dc, [2dctog] 3 times, 1 dc in each of next 23 dc, 2 dc in 2nd ch. [97 sts.]

All sizes

[79 (85:91:97) sts.] Incs at front edges for collar have been completed.

Next row: 1 sc in 1st dc, 2 ch, 1 dc in each of next 18 (20:22:24) dc, [2dctog] twice, 1 dc in each of next 5 dc, [2dctog] twice, 1 dc in each of next 15 (17:19:21) dc, [2dctog] twice, 1 dc in each of next 5 dc, [2dctog] twice, 1 dc in each of next 18 (20:22:24) dc, 1 dc in 2nd ch. [71 (77:83:89) sts.]

Next row: 1 sc in 1st dc, 2 ch, 1 dc in each of

next 17 (19:21:23) dc, [2dctog] twice, 1 dc in
each of next 3 dc, [2dctog] twice, 1 dc in each
of next 13 (15:17:19) dc, [2dctog] twice, 1 dc
in each of next 3 dc, [2dctog] twice, 1 dc in
each of next 17 (19:21:23) dc, 1 dc in 2nd ch.
[63 (69:75:81) sts.]
Next row: 1 sc in 1st dc, 2 ch, 1 dc in each of
next 16 (18:20:22) dc, [2dctog] twice, 1 dc in
next dc, [2dctog] twice, 1 dc in each of next
11 (13:15:17) dc, [2dctog] twice, 1 dc in next
dc, [2dctog] twice, 1 dc in each of next 16
(18:20:22) dc, 1 dc in 2nd ch. [55 (61:67:73) sts.]
Cont in dc, work 11 rows. Fasten off.

EDGING

With WS facing, join yarn at lower edge of left
front. Spacing picots evenly, work up left front
edge, along collar edge and down right front
edge.
Picot row: 1 sc, 3 ch, sl st in side of last sc,
[2 sc, 3 ch, sl st in side of last sc] to end.

TIE BELT (OPTIONAL)

Make 65 (66:67:68) picots and work Row 1 as
given for back and fronts. Work picot row as
given for edging into Row 1. Fasten off.

FINISHING

Taking one st from each edge into seam, join
sleeve seams. Join underarm seams. Try on
coat and mark position for belt loops. Make a
loop of crochet chain for each belt loop.

This artful wrap will add a bright touch to any outfit. The pretty trefoil pattern is worked primarily in chain with the simple flowers and tassels added last.

TASSEL-EDGED WRAP

★☆☆ BEGINNER

HELPFUL HINT

- The flower motifs are easy to do once you're confident about working different height stitches. Here's a reminder of how many times to take the yarn around the hook at beginning: sc = zero times, hdc = once but pull through all loops first time; dc = once; tr = twice, dtr = 3 times.

MEASUREMENTS

Actual width
15 in
38 cm
Actual length
75 in
190 cm

MATERIALS

- 7 × 50 g balls of Debbie Bliss Merino DK in yellow 503
- F/5 (3.75 mm) crochet hook

GAUGE

One repeat measures 2½ in (6.5 cm). 10 rows to 4 in (10 cm) measured over trefoil chain pattern, each flower motif measures 3 in (7.5 cm) across, both when pressed, using F/5 (3.75 mm) hook. Change hook size if necessary to obtain this gauge.

ABBREVIATIONS

See page 9.

WRAP

Row 1 (WS): 16 ch, sl st in 8th ch from hook, [7ch, sl st in same ch as last sl st] twice, * 23 ch, sl st in 8th ch from hook, [7 ch, sl st in same ch as last sl st] twice, rep from * until there are 23 trefoil chain motifs, 8 ch, turn.
Row 2: Make 7 more ch, sl st in 8th ch from hook, 7 ch, sl st in same ch as last sl st, 7 ch, 1 sc in 2nd 7 ch loop of next trefoil, * 7 ch, skip 7 ch on Row 1, sl st in next ch, [7 ch, sl st in same ch as last sl st] 3 times, 7 ch, 1 sc in 2nd 7 ch loop of next trefoil, rep from * to last 8 ch, 7 ch, sl st in last ch of Row 1, 7 ch, sl st in same ch as last sl st, 4 ch, 1 tr in same ch as last sl st, turn.
Row 3: 1 ch, 1 sc in tr, * 7 ch, sl st in next sc, [7 ch, sl st in same sc as last sl st] 3 times, 7 ch, 1 sc in 2nd 7 ch loop, rep from * to end, turn.
Row 4: [7 ch, sl st in 1st sc] twice, 7 ch, 1 sc in 2nd 7 ch loop, * 7 ch, sl st in next sc, [7 ch, sl st in same sc as last sl st] 3 times, 7 ch, 1 sc in 2nd 7 ch loop, rep from * to last sc, [7 ch, sl st in last sc] twice, 4 ch, 1 tr in last sc, turn.
Rows 3 and 4 form the pattern.
Work 17 more rows, so ending with a 3rd patt row. Fasten off.

The starting chain for the trefoil chain pattern forms the first row and part of the second row.

Picking out the repeat to check your gauge over the trefoil chain pattern can be difficult, so start by working a flower motif. If it is the right size, you've got the first one done (except for pulling back the last half petal to join) and your gauge over the trefoil chain should be correct too.

FLOWER MOTIF

To form ring, wind yarn around index finger of left hand, insert hook, yo and pull through. Work over end as well as into ring, then before joining on 1st round, pull end to tighten. Weave in end securely before trimming it off.

First motif

Round 1 (RS): 2 ch, work 12 sc in ring, sl st in 1st sc.

Round 2: 3 ch, 1 dc in next sc, [2 ch, 1 dc in each of next 2 sc] 5 times, 2 ch, sl st in 3rd ch.

Round 3: Sl st in 1st dc, * [1 sc, 1 hdc, 1 dc, 1 tr, 1 dtr, 1 ch, 1 dtr, 1 tr, 1 dc, 1 hdc, 1 sc] all in next 2 ch space, rep from * 4 more times, in last 2 ch space, work 1 sc, 1 hdc, 1 dc, 1 tr, 1 dtr, with WS of wrap and flower motif together work 1 sc in center 7 ch loop of first trefoil motif along lower edge of wrap, 1 dtr, 1 tr, 1 dc, 1 hdc, 1 sc in last 2 ch space, sl st in 1st sc. Fasten off.

2nd and following motifs

Work as given for 1st motif until 4 petals of Round 3 have been completed. Join 5th petal with 1 sc in 1 ch space at center of 1st petal of previous flower motif and 6th petal to next trefoil motif of wrap.

Continue until all trefoil motifs have a flower motif attached. Make 3 more flowers, joining first one at corner and to adjacent flower, then second to edge and first flower, work third flower until 3 petals have been completed, join 4th petal to corner of wrap, 5th petal to edge and 6th petal to 2nd flower. Work 3 more flowers for the other short edge.

Use nine 9½ in (24-cm) lengths of yarn folded in half plus a longer length to knot, wrap top to make a tassel for each flower. Use long end to sew tassels to flowers. Press. Trim tassels.

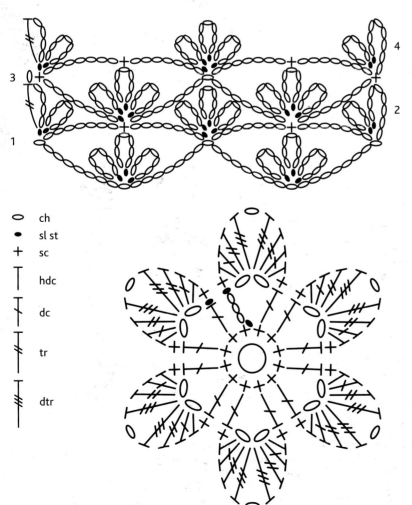

Symbol	Stitch
○	ch
●	sl st
+	sc
T	hdc
⊤	dc
⊤	tr
⊤	dtr

CASUAL

There are times when you need a little stay-at-home, slouchy chic. The garments in this section are all about enjoying the feel of the yarns as you work the projects and the touch of the fabric when you wear the garments you've created. Luxuriate in the thick velvety surface of the chenille cowl or feel the contrast between soft cotton and silky ribbon in the tank top. Go for the gentle texture of the nubbly yarn used for the simple sweater, cover up in a bell-shaped, wool poncho, or for a sophisticated take on the casual look, choose the cardigan with ruffled edge in a creamy soft cashmere mix yarn.

This mini poncho is just a simple tube collar that increases out around the shoulders and ends in a fringe. Wear it indoors over a little top or layer it over a coat or jacket when outdoors.

CHENILLE COWL

BEGINNER

Do not count the 1 ch at the beginning of each round as a stitch.

Work the foundation chain loosely.

Handle the yarn gently, coaxing the loops through quite loosely as you form the stitches. If you pull hard, the core of the yarn will lock and the stitches will be uneven or the yarn could break.

To join in new yarn, simply twist the ends together close to the work so the core at the center of the yarn meets and links. To weave in the ends, strip off the velvet pile, knot the ends close to the join and weave in the remaining threads.

HELPFUL HINTS

- Wow! is a chunky, velvety chenille yarn. Knot the yarn end before you start to crochet to prevent shedding. Snip off the knots to weave in the ends.
- The cowl is worked in rounds so there is no sewing up – simply weave in the ends and it's ready to wear!

MEASUREMENTS

One size
Actual measurement around neck edge
21½ in
55 cm
Actual measurement around lower edge
43¼ in
110 cm
Actual length (without fringe)
13¾ in
35 cm

MATERIALS

- 1 × 100 g ball of Sirdar Wow! in each of Cream Soda 755 (A), Pale Chamois 759 (B) and Light Suede 757 (C)
- N/15 (10.00 mm) crochet hook

GAUGE

6 sts and 6 rows to 4 in (10 cm) measured over single crochet worked in rounds using N/15 (10.00 mm) hook. Change hook size if necessary to obtain this gauge.

ABBREVIATIONS

See page 9.

COWL

Using A, make 33 ch, sl st in 1st ch to form a ring.
Round 1: 1 ch, 1 sc in each ch to end, sl st in 1st sc. [33 sts.]
Round 2: 1 ch, 1 sc in each sc to end, sl st in 1st sc. This round forms sc.
Cont in sc, work 8 more rounds.
Inc round 1: 1 ch, 1 sc in 1st sc, [2 sc in next sc, 1 sc in each of 2 foll sc] 10 times, 2 sc in next sc, 1 sc in foll sc, sl st in 1st sc. [44 sts.]
Change to B. Work 3 rounds sc.
Inc round 2: 1 ch, 1 sc in 1st sc, [2 sc in next sc, 1 sc in foll sc] 21 times, 2 sc in last sc, sl st in 1st sc. [66 sts.]
Cont in sc, work 3 more rounds.
Change to C. Work 3 rounds sc.
Fringe round: Using your fingers, pull a 4-in (10-cm) loop through first sc, from back to front of work and take yarn around base of loop close to edge, finish each sc around edge with a loop. Cut yarn. Weave in end securely.

FINISHING

Gently pull on each fringe loop to even out the twists. Weave in remaining ends. Roll collar down.

This simple tank top is deceivingly easy to make. Its striking pattern is made from one band of contrast color across the bodice. Random changes of matte and shiny textures in the ribbon yarn create a complex patchwork of contrasting shapes.

SHIMMERY TANK TOP

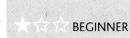 *This is one of the simplest garments to make, with no sleeve seams to match up and worked in simple stitches.*

HELPFUL HINTS
- Ribbon yarn can unravel if the end is pulled. To prevent this, tie a knot in the end before starting to crochet. Snip off the knots before weaving in the ends.
- The patterned effect will be different for each tank top because of the random nature of the changes in color

MEASUREMENTS
To fit bust

32	34	36	38	40	42	in
81	86	91	97	102	107	cm

Actual width

32½	34½	36½	38¾	41	43	in
82.5	88	93	98.5	104	109	cm

Actual length

18¼	18¾	19	20½	21	21¼	in
46.5	47.5	48.5	52	53	54	cm

In the instructions, figures are given for the smallest size first; larger sizes follow in parentheses. Where only one set of figures is given this applies to all sizes.

MATERIALS
- 4 (4:5:5:6:6) × 50 g balls of Sirdar Duet in Ivory 744 (A)
- 1 (1:1:2:2:2) × 50 g balls of Sirdar Duet in Chamois 741 (B)
- G/6 (4.00 mm) crochet hook

GAUGE
15 sts and 9 rows to 4 in (10 cm) measured over double crochet patt using G/6 (4.00 mm) hook. Change hook size if necessary to obtain this gauge.

ABBREVIATIONS
3dctog – leaving last loop of each st on hook, work a double crochet in each of next 3 sts, yo and pull through 4 loops on hook
See also page 9.

TOP

BACK
Using A, make 64 (68:72:76:80:84) ch.
Row 1 (WS): Work 1 dc in 4th ch from hook, 1 dc in each ch to end.
[62 (66:70:74:78:82) sts.]
Row 2: 1 sc in 1st dc, 2 ch, 1 dc in each dc to last st, 1 dc in 3rd ch.
This row forms dc patt.
Working into 2nd ch at end of foll rows, cont in dc, work 14 more rows.
Change to B. Work 7 (7:7:8:8:8) rows.
Change to A. Work 2 (2:2:3:3:3) rows.

Shape armholes
Next row (RS): Sl st in each of first 3 dc, 1 sc in next dc, 2 ch, 1 dc in each dc to last 3 sts, turn. [56 (60:64:68:72:76) sts.]

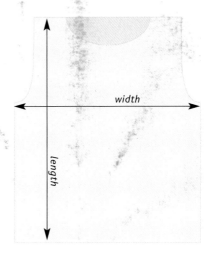

width

length

Dec row: 1 sc in 1st dc, 2 ch, 3dctog, 1 dc in each dc to last 4 sts, 3dctog, 1 dc in 2nd ch. [52 (56:60:64:68:72) sts.]
Cont in dc, dec two sts in this way at each end of next 1 (2:2:2:3:3) rows.
[48 (48:52:56:56:60) sts **.]
Cont in dc, work 14 (14:15:16:16:17) rows. Fasten off.

FRONT

Work as given for back to **.
Cont in dc, work 4 (4:5:6:6:7) rows.

Shape neck

Next row: 1 sc in 1st dc, 2 ch, 1 dc in each of next 17 (17:18:20:20:21) dc, turn and complete first side on these 18 (18:19:21:21:22) sts. Cont in dc, dec 2 sts by working 3dctog one st in from neck edge on next 4 rows. [10 (10:11:13:13:14) sts.]
Work 5 rows even. Fasten off. Leave center 12 (12:14:14:14:16) dc, join yarn in next dc, 3 ch, 1 dc in each dc to end.
[18 (18:19:21:21:22) sts.]
Complete to match first side.

FINISHING

Matching sts, join shoulders.

Neck edging

With RS facing, join A at right shoulder. Work 1 sc in first dc of back neck, 2 ch, 1 dc in each of 27 (27:29:29:29:31) dc across back neck, 19 dc in row-ends down left front neck, 1 dc in each of 12 (12:14:14:14:16) dc across front neck and 19 dc in row-ends up right front neck, sl st in 2nd ch. Fasten off.

Armhole edgings

With RS facing, join A to first dc at underarm. Work 1 sc in first dc, 2 ch, 1 dc in each of next 2 dc, 34 (36:38:40:42:44) dc in row-ends to shoulder, 1 dc in seam, 34 (36:38:40:42:44) dc in row ends to underarm and 1 dc in each of next 3 sts. Fasten off.
Join side and armhole edging seams.

This skinny-fit sweater is worked in simple double crochet. The softly textured yarn creates a rich, textured effect. And because it is stretchy, it creates a close-fitting garment.

SIMPLE TEXTURED SWEATER

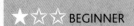 *When shaping the sleeves, place markers at each end of every inc row to make it easier to keep track of the number of incs worked. The markers will also help match the row-ends when sewing up.*

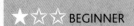 *Sewing up with textured yarn is simple if you have the RS of the work facing, and use mattress stitch and a blunt-pointed needle.*

HELPFUL HINTS

- The yarn alternates between thin, smooth threads and soft, furry nubs. Textured yarns can be difficult to work with but this one is easy because the hook catches the smooth parts of the yarn neatly and the thicker bits pull through easily.

MEASUREMENTS

To fit bust

32	34	36	38	40	in
81	86	91	97	102	cm

Actual bust

32	34½	36¾	39½	41¾	in
81	87.5	93.5	100	106	cm

Actual length

20½	21	21¼	21½	22	in
52	53	54	55	56	cm

Actual sleeve

18 in
46 cm

In the instructions, figures are given for the smallest size first; larger sizes follow in parentheses. Where only one set of figures is given this applies to all sizes.

MATERIALS

- 8 (9:10:11:12) × 50 g balls of Sirdar Fresco in Faded Denim 804
- F/5 (3.75 mm) crochet hook

GAUGE

16 sts and 10 rows to 4 in (10 cm) over double crochet using F/5 (3.75 mm) hook. Change hook size if necessary to obtain this gauge.

ABBREVIATIONS

2dctog – leaving last loop of each st on hook, work a double crochet in each of next 2 sts, yo and pull through 3 loops on hook
3dctog – leaving last loop of each st on hook, work a double crochet in each of next 3 sts, yo and pull through 4 loops on hook
See also page 9.

SWEATER

BACK

Make 61 (66:71:76:81) ch.
Row 1 (WS): 1 dc in 4th ch from hook, 1 dc in each ch to end. [59 (64:69:74:79) sts.]
Row 2: 3 ch, skip 1st dc, 1 dc in each dc to last st, 1 dc in 3rd ch.
Row 2 forms double crochet. Cont in dc work 19 more rows.
Inc row (RS): 3 ch, 1 dc in 1st dc usually skipped, 1 dc in each dc to last st, 2 dc in 3rd ch. [61 (66:71:76:81) sts.]
Cont in dc, inc in this way at each end of next 2 RS rows. [65 (70:75:80:85) sts.]
Cont in dc, work 7 rows.

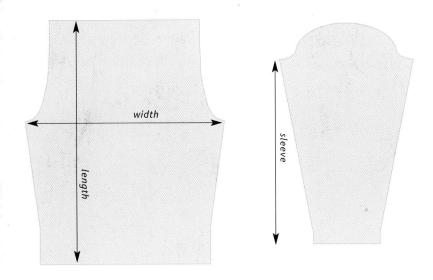

Shape armholes

Next row (RS): Sl st in each of 1st 3 dc, 3 ch, skip dc with last sl st, 1 dc in each dc to last 2 sts, turn. [61 (66:71:76:81) sts.]

Dec row: 3 ch, skip 1st dc, 2dctog, 1 dc in each dc to last 2 sts, 2dctog. [59 (64:69:74:79) sts.] Cont in dc dec in this way at each end of next 5 (6:6:7:7) rows. [49 (52:57:60:65) sts **.] Cont in dc, work 12 (12:13:13:14) rows. Fasten off.

FRONT

Work as given for back to **. Cont in tr, work 8 (8:9:9:10) rows.

Shape neck

Next row: 3 ch, skip 1st dc, 1 dc in each of next 13 (14:15:16:18) dc, turn and complete right side on these 14 (15:16:17:19) sts. Cont in dc, dec by working 2dctog at neck edge on next 3 rows. [11 (12:13:14:16) sts.] Fasten off. Leave center 21 (22:25:26:27) dc, join yarn in next dc, 3 ch, skip dc joined into, 1 dc in each st to end. [14 (15:16:17:19) sts.] Cont in dc, dec by working 2dctog at neck edge on next 3 rows. [11 (12:13:14:16) sts.] Fasten off.

SLEEVES (MAKE 2)

Make 28 (30:34:36:40) ch.

Row 1 (WS): 1 dc in 4th ch from hook, 1 dc in each ch to end. [26 (28:32:34:38) sts.]

Row 2: 3 ch, skip 1st dc, 1 dc in each dc to last st, 1 dc in 3rd ch.

Row 2 forms double crochet. Cont in dc, work 3 more rows. Inc in same way as back at each end of next row and on 13 foll 3rd rows. [54 (56:60:62:66) sts.] Work 1 row.

Shape top

Next row: Sl st in each of 1st 3 dc, 3 ch, skip dc with last sl st, 1 dc in each dc to last 2 sts, turn. [50 (52:56:58:62) sts.] Cont in dc dec in same way as back at each end of next 6 (7:7:8:8) rows. [38 (38:42:42:46) sts.]

Next row: 3 ch, skip 1st dc, 3dctog, 1 dc in each dc to last 3 sts, 3dctog. [34 (34:38:38:42) sts.] Work last row 1 (1:2:2:3) more times. [30 sts.] Fasten off.

NECKBAND

Matching sts, join shoulders. With RS facing, join yarn in 1st dc of back neck, 3 ch, 1 dc in each of next 26 (27:30:31:32) dc across back neck, 10 dc in row-ends down left front neck, 1 dc in each of 21 (22:25:26:27) dc across front neck, 10 dc in row-ends up right front neck, sl st in 3rd ch. [68 (70:76:78:80) sts.] Turn. 3 ch, skip 1st dc, 1 dc in each dc to end, sl st in 3rd ch. Fasten off.

FINISHING

Set in sleeves. Join side and sleeve seams.

VARIATION

SPORTY HEADBAND

Make a fashionable, sporty headband using any leftover yarn, or the same yarn in a contrasting color. Make 12 ch.

Row 1 (WS): 1 dc in 4th ch from hook, 1 dc in each ch to end. [10 sts.]

Row 2: 3 ch, skip 1st dc, 1 dc in each dc to last st, 1 dc in 3rd ch. 2nd row forms double crochet. Cont in dc, working until band, when slightly stretched, fits around head. Fasten off. Join ends.

This pretty poncho is made from eight-sided motifs joined in rounds to give a bell shape that curves over the shoulders and falls in a soft drape to the hips.

FLOWER MOTIF PONCHO

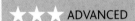 *Instructions are given to work all the motifs and then join them. If you prefer, you can join the motifs and work the edging each time you complete enough motifs to make a round.*

Always weave in the end from the starting ring, don't just snip it off.

Save time and weave in ends as you go.

HELPFUL HINTS

- If you are really short of time you can make a simpler, shorter version of the poncho, like a little shoulder cape. You'll only need to crochet 24 motifs, then finish the poncho after assembling the first and second rounds of motifs. You'll need just 5 balls of yarn.

MEASUREMENTS

One size
Actual length
21¼ in
54 cm

MATERIALS

- 10 × 50 g balls of Debbie Bliss Merino DK in Pink 615
- E/4 (3.50 mm) crochet hook

GAUGE

Each motif measures 3¾ in (9.5 cm), when pressed, using E/4 (3.50 mm) hook. Change hook size if necessary to obtain this size motif.

ABBREVIATIONS

3dtrcl – leaving last loop of each st on hook, work 3dtr, yo and pull through 4 loops on hook *See also page 9.*

PONCHO

FLOWER OCTAGON MOTIF

Wind yarn around first finger to form a ring.
Round 1 (RS): 5 ch, leaving last loop of each st on hook, work 2 dtr in ring, yo and pull through 3 loops on hook, [5 ch, 3dtrcl in ring] 7 times, 2 ch, 1 dc in 5th ch, pull end to tighten ring.
Round 2: 1 ch, 1 sc in first sp, 6 ch, [1 sc in next 5 ch sp, 6 ch] 7 times, sl st in 1st sc.
Round 3: Sl st in first 6 ch sp, 3 ch, 6 dc in first 6 ch sp, 3 ch [7 dc in next 6 ch cp, 3 ch] 7 times, sl st in 3rd ch. Fasten off.

Make 56 flower octagon motifs.

Join 1st line of 8 motifs

With RS together, join two motifs by working 1 sc into 3 ch sp, 1 sc into each of the 7 dc along one edge, 1 sc in 3 ch sp. Open out motifs and leaving one edge at top for neckline and 5 edges below free, continue to join 6 more motifs in the same way, then join 8th motif to 7th, then to 1st to form a ring.

Join 2nd line of 16 motifs

Join 2 motifs in same way as 1st line of motifs. Open out motifs and leaving 3 edges at each side, continue to join 14 more motifs in the same way, then join 16th motif to 15th, then to 1st to form a ring.

Join 3rd and 4th lines of motifs

Join 16 motifs in same way as 2nd line of motifs.

Lower edge of 1st line of motifs

Join yarn in last free 3 ch sp of 8th joined motif at lower edge of 1st line of motifs.

Round 1 (RS): 1 ch, 3 sc in same 3 ch sp as joined yarn, ** 3 sc in 1st 3 ch sp of next motif, 3 ch, * skip 1 dc, [1 dc in next dc, 1 ch, skip 1 dc] 3 times, work [1 dc, 1 ch] twice in next 3 ch sp, rep from * once, skip 1 dc, [1 dc in next dc, 1 ch, skip 1 dc] 3 times, work 2 more ch, 3 sc in last 3 ch sp of this motif, rep from ** 7 times, omitting last 3 sc of last rep, sl st in 1st sc.

Round 2: 4 ch, skip 4 sc, 1 tr in next sc, 3 ch, * 1 tr in 1st dc, [1 tr in next sp, 1 tr in next dc] 12 times **, yo 4 times, insert hook in 1st sc of next 3 sc group, yo and pull loop through [yo and pull through 2 loops on hook] twice, yo twice, insert hook in last sc of foll 3 sc group, yo and pull loop through, [yo and pull through 2 loops on hook] twice, yo and pull through 3 loops on hook, [yo and pull through 2 loops on hook] twice, rep from * 6 more times, then work from * to **, sl st in 3rd ch. [208 sts.]

Round 3: 4 ch, skip 1 tr, [1 dc in next st, 1 ch, skip one st] to end, sl st in 3rd ch.

Join edging and 2nd line of motifs

Round 1: 1 ch, 1 sc in same place as sl st, 1 sc in next sp, 1 sc in next dc, with RS tog, join top edge of 1st motif of 2nd line of motifs with sc by working * 2 sps tog, [next dc from each edge tog, foll sp and dc tog] 3 times, then work next dc from each edge tog and foll 2 sps tog *, 1 sc in next dc, 1 sc in next sp, 1 sc in next dc, rep from * to * to join 2nd motif, [1 sc in next dc, 1 sc in next sp] twice, 1 sc in foll dc, cont joining motifs, working 5 sc and 3 sc alternately in edge between joining motifs until all 16 motifs have been joined ending 1 sc in last dc, 1 sc in last sp, sl st in 1st sc. Fasten off.

Lower edge of 2nd line of motifs

Join yarn to 2nd dc of 1st motif.

Round 1: 4 ch, * [skip one st, 1 dc in next dc or sp, 1 ch] 10 times, 1 dc in 2nd dc of next motif, 1 ch, rep from * to end, omitting last dc and ch, sl st in 3rd ch. Fasten off.

Join yarn in 3rd sp of Round 1.

Round 2: 4 ch, * [1 tr in next dc, 1 tr in next sp] 5 times, yo 4 times, skip one sp, insert hook in next sp, yo and pull loop through, [yo and pull through 2 loops on hook] twice, yo twice, skip one sp, insert hook in foll sp, yo and pull loop through [yo and pull through 2 loops on hook] twice, yo and pull through 3 loops on hook, [yo and pull through 2 loops on hook] twice, skip one sp, 1 tr in next sp,

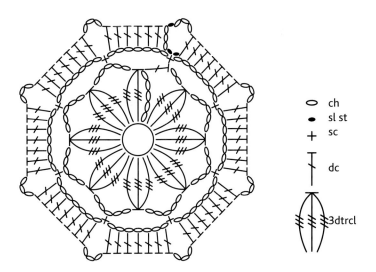

○	ch
●	sl st
+	sc
┬	dc
	3dtrcl

rep from * to end, omitting last tr, sl st in 4th ch.

Round 3: 4 ch, [1 dc in next tr, 1 ch] to end, sl st in 3rd ch. Fasten off.

Join yarn in 5th sp from end of Round 3.

Join edging and 3rd line of motifs

Round 1: 1 ch, with RS tog, join top edge of 1st motif of 3rd line of motifs with sc by working * 2 sps tog, [next dc and sp tog] 7 times, then work foll 2 sps tog, 2 sc in each of next 3 sps, rep from * to end, sl st in 1st sc. Fasten off.

Lower edge of 3rd line of motifs

Work 3 rounds as given for lower edge of 2nd line of motifs.

Join edging and 4th line of motifs

Work as given for join edging and 3rd line of motifs.

Lower edge of 4th line of motifs

Work 3 rounds as given for lower edge of 2nd line of motifs but turn instead of fastening off after Round 3.

Round 4: 1 ch, 2 sc in each sp to end, sl st in 1st sc. Fasten off.

COLLAR

With RS facing, join yarn to a 3 ch sp at beg of a motif at top edge of 1st line of motifs.

Round 1 (RS): 4 ch, skip 1st dc, [1 dc in next dc, 1 ch, skip next dc] 3 times, [1 dc in 3 ch sp, 1 ch] twice, rep from * 7 more times, omitting last dc and ch, sl st in 3rd ch.

Round 2: 4 ch, 1 tr in 1st 1 ch sp, [1 tr in next dc, 1 tr in next sp] to end, sl st in 4th ch. [80 sts.]

Round 3: 4 ch, 1 tr in each tr to end, sl st in 4th ch.

Cont in tr, work 6 more rounds. Fasten off.

FINISHING

Weave in ends. Press according to ball band. Roll collar down.

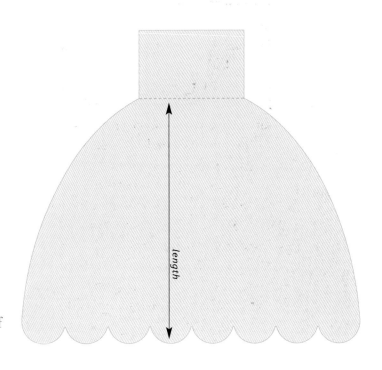

This soft, supple cashmere blend yarn is a joy to handle. It gives an exquisite quality to the easy-to-work, single and double crochet stitch pattern used for this sophisticated but simple cardigan.

CARDIGAN WITH RUFFLED EDGE

★★☆ MEDIUM

Work the foundation chain quite loosely. If necessary, use one size larger hook.

Instead of the usual 3 ch, a sc and 2 ch are worked at the start of each double crochet row to close the gap between the first and second stitches. Stretch the loop on the hook slightly before making the sc.

The 1 ch at the start of a sc row does not count as a stitch.

HELPFUL HINTS
- Keep your work clean by storing it in a pillow case.

MEASUREMENTS
To fit bust

32	34	36	38	40	42	44	in
81	86	91	97	102	107	112	cm

Actual bust

35	37½	39¾	42	44½	47¼	49½	in
89	95	101	107	113	120	126	cm

Actual length

24	24	24½	24½	25¼	25¼	26	in
60.5	60.5	62.5	62.5	64.5	64.5	66	cm

Actual sleeve
19 in
48 cm

In the instructions, figures are given for the smallest size first; larger sizes follow in parentheses. Where only one set of figures is given this applies to all sizes.

MATERIALS
- 15 (16:16:17:18:18:19) × 50 g balls of Debbie Bliss Cashmerino Aran in 101
- H/8 (5.00 mm) crochet hook

GAUGE
13 sts and 11 rows to 4 in (10 cm) measured over single crochet and double crochet pattern using H/8 (5.00 mm) hook. Change hook size if necessary to obtain this gauge.

ABBREVIATIONS
3dctog – leaving last loop of each st on hook, work a double crochet in each of next 3 sts, yo and pull through 4 loops on hook
See also page 9.

CARDIGAN

BACK
Make 51 (55:59:63:67:71:75) ch.
Row 1 (WS): 1 sc in 2nd ch from hook, 1 sc in each ch to end. [50 (54:58:62:66:70:74) sts.]
Row 2: 1 sc in 1st sc, 2 ch, 1 dc in each sc to end.
Row 3: 1 ch, 1 sc in each dc to last st, 1 sc in 2nd ch.
Rows 2 and 3 form sc and dc patt. Cont in patt, work 20 more rows, ending with a 3rd patt row.
Inc row (RS): 1 sc in 1st sc, 2 ch, 1 dc in 1st sc, 1 dc in each sc to last sc, 2 dc in last sc. [52 (56:60:64:68:72:76) sts.]
Cont in patt, inc in this way at each end of 3 foll 6th rows. [58 (62:66:70:74:78:82) sts.]
Cont in patt, work 3 rows, ending with a 3rd patt row.

Shape armholes

Next row: (RS) Sl st in each of first 3 (3:4:4:5:5:6) dc, 3 ch, skip sc with sl st, 1 dc in each sc to last 2 (2:3:3:4:4:5) sc, turn. [54 (58:60:64:66:70:72) sts.] Patt 1 row.

Dec row: 1 sc in first sc, 2 ch, 3dctog, 1 dc in each sc to last 4 sts, 3dctog, 1 dc in last sc. [50 (54:56:60:62:66:68) sts.]

Patt 1 row. Work dec row again. [46 (50:52:56:58:62:64) sts.]

Patt 1 row. Work dec row again. [42 (46:48:52:54:58:60) sts.]

Patt 15 (15:17:17:19:19:21) rows, ending with a 3rd patt row. Fasten off.

LEFT FRONT

Make 33 (35:37:39:41:43:45) ch.

Row 1 (WS): 1 sc in 2nd ch from hook, 1 sc in each ch to end. [32 (34:36:38:40:42:44) sts.]

Row 2: 1 sc in 1st sc, 2 ch, 1 dc in each sc to end.

Row 3: 1 ch, 1 sc in each dc to last st, 1 sc in 2nd ch.

Rows 2 and 3 form sc and dc patt. Cont in patt, work 20 more rows, ending with a 3rd patt row **.

Inc row (RS): 1 sc in 1st sc, 2 ch, 1 dc in 1st sc, 1 dc in each sc to end. [33 (35:37:39:41:43:45) sts.]

Cont in patt, inc in this way at beg of 3 foll 6th rows. [36 (38:40:42:44:46:48) sts.] Cont in patt, work 3 rows, ending with a 3rd patt row.

Shape armhole

Next row (RS): Sl st in each of first 3 (3:4:4:5:5:6) sc, 3 ch, skip sc with sl st, 1 dc in each sc to end. [34 (36:37:39:40:42:43) sts.] Patt 1 row.

Dec row: 1 sc in first sc, 2 ch, 3dctog, 1 dc in each sc to end. [32 (34:35:37:38:40:41) sts.] Patt 1 row. Work dec row again. [30 (32:33:35:36:38:39) sts.] Patt 1 row. Work dec row again. [28 (30:31:33:34:36:37) sts.] Patt 9 (9:11:11:13:13:15) rows, ending with a 3rd patt row.

Shape neck

Row 1 (RS): 1 dc in 1st sc, 2 ch, 1 dc in each of next 8 (10:11:12:13:14:15) sc, 3dctog, 1 dc in next sc, turn and leave 15 (15:15:16:16:17:17) dc for neck. [11 (13:14:15:16:17:18) sts.] Patt 1 row.

Row 3: 1 sc in 1st sc, 2 ch, 1 dc in each sc to last 4 sc, 3dctog, 1 dc in last sc. [9 (11:12:13:14:15:16) sts.] Patt 3 rows. Fasten off.

RIGHT FRONT

Work as given for Left Front to **.

Inc row (RS): 1 sc in 1st sc, 2 ch, 1 dc in each sc to last sc, 2 dc in last sc. [33 (35:37:39:41:43:45) sts.] Cont in patt, inc in this way at end of 3 foll 6th rows. [36 (38:40:42:44:46:48) sts.] Cont in patt, work 3 rows, ending with a 3rd patt row.

Shape armhole

Next row (RS): 1 sc in 1st sc, 2 ch, 1 dc in each sc to last 2 (2:3:3:4:4:5) sc, turn. [34 (36:37:39:40:42:43) sts.] Patt 1 row.

Dec row (RS): 1 sc in first sc, 2 ch, 1 dc in each sc to last 4 sts, 3dctog, 1 dc in last sc. [32 (34:35:37:38:40:41) sts.] Patt 1 row. Work dec row again. [30 (32:33:35:36:38:39) sts.] Patt 1 row. Work dec row again. [28 (30:31:33:34:36:37) sts.] Patt 9 (9:11:11:13:13:15) rows, ending with a 3rd patt row. Fasten off. With RS facing, leave first 15 (15:15:16:16:17:17) sc for neck.

Shape neck

Row 1 (RS): Join yarn and work 1 sc in next sc, 2 ch, 3dctog, 1 dc in each sc to end. [11 (13:14:15:16:17:18) sts.] Patt 1 row.

Row 3: 1 sc in 1st sc, 2 ch, 3dctog, 1 dc in each sc to end. [9 (11:12:13:14:15:16) sts.] Patt 3 rows. Fasten off.

SLEEVES (MAKE 2)

Make 31 (31:31:35:35:39:39) ch.

Row 1 (WS): 1 sc in 2nd ch from hook, 1 sc in each ch to end. [30 (30:30:34:34:38:38) sts.] Work in sc and dc patt as given for back for 4 rows. Cont in patt, inc in same way as back at each end of next row and on 6 (7:7:7:7:7:7) foll 6th rows. [44 (46:46:50:50:54:54) sts.]

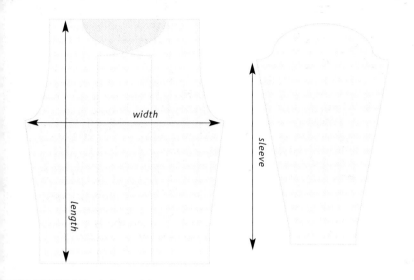

If you'd like just a small shell edging, finish the fronts and neck edge with Row 1 and Row 6 of front and neck edging as given for the cuffs. If you do this, you'll need one less ball of yarn.

Inc at each end of next 0 (0:1:0:1:0:2) RS rows. [44 (46:48:50:52:54:58) sts.] Patt 11 (5:3:5:3:5:1) rows.

Shape top

Next row (RS): Sl st in each of first 3 (3:4:4:5:5:6) sc, 3 ch, skip sc with sl st, 1 dc in each sc to last 2 (2:3:3:4:4:5) sc, turn. [40 (42:42:44:44:46:48) sts.] Patt 1 row.

Dec row: 1 sc in first sc, 2 ch, 3dctog, 1 dc in each sc to last 4 sts, 3dctog, 1 dc in last sc. [36 (38:38:40:40:42:44) sts.] Dec in this way at each end of next 6 RS rows. [12 (14:14:16:16:18:20) sts.] Patt 1 (1:3:1:3:1:3) rows. Fasten off.

EDGINGS

Preparation for front and neck edging

Matching sts, join shoulders. With WS facing, work 87 (87:91:91:95:95:99) sc up left front edge to beginning of neck shaping. Fasten off. Starting at neck edge, work 86 (86:90:90:94:94:98) sc along right front edge. Fasten off. With WS of left front facing, join yarn after 15 (15:15:16:16:17:17) sc at neck and work 9 sc around shaped edge to shoulder. Fasten off. Starting at shoulder, work right front neck to match.

Front and neck edging

Row 1 (RS): Join yarn with a sc in 1st sc of right front edge, * [skip 1 sc, 4 dc in next sc, skip 1 sc, 1 sc in next sc] * 21 (21:22:22: 23:23:24) times up right front edge, skip 1 sc, 4 dc in corner sc, skip 1 sc, 1 sc in next sc, rep from * to * 17 (17:17:18:18:19:19) times around neck edge, skip 1 sc, 4 dc in corner sc, skip 1 sc, 1 sc in next sc, rep from * to * 21 (21:22:22:23:23:24) times down left front edge.

Rows 2 and 4: 1 ch, 1 sc in each st to end.

Row 3: 1 sc in 1st sc, 2 ch, 1 dc in same dc, [2 dc in each sc] to end.

Row 5: 1 sc in 1st sc, 2 ch, [1 dc in each sc] to end, do not turn.

Row 6 (RS): Working from left to right, work 1 sc in each st. Fasten off.

FINISHING

Press according to ball band. Set in sleeves. Taking one st in from each edge, join side and sleeve seams.

Cuff edging

With RS facing join yarn with a sc in sleeve seam and work around edge as given for Row 1 of front and neck edging, then work Row 6 of front and neck edging. Fasten off.

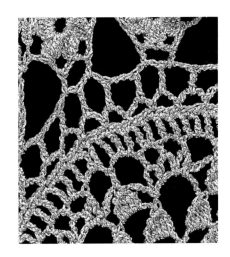

GLAMOROUS

When it's party time, crochet comes into the spotlight. Whether your personal style is full-on glitz or you just want to spark up a plain outfit, you'll find something special here. Create an unforgettable image with the stunning, vintage-look circular vest or dazzle them in the sparkle of a sequin-trimmed tank top. Layer the long pointed-edge vest over trousers or a dress. Keep your shoulders cozy with a fabulous ruffled wrap in fine mohair, the shell-edged shrug in angora-mix yarn or the faux fur blue capelet. And for a touch of shine, day or night, add the slender, beaded gold scarf to any outfit.

GOLD CIRCLE VEST

This unusually long vest is made from a huge circle of lacy crochet. Worked in fine metallic yarn, the filagree of stitches gives the vest a vintage feel.

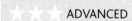 *The back and fronts of the vest are worked in one big circle, starting from the center back and working in rounds. Spaces are left for the armholes, then the circle is continued to form the fronts and collar.*

When working 3 or more chains to stand for a stitch at the start of a round, make the last chain slightly loose so it's easier to work the slip stitch under both strands of the loop when joining the round.

Weave in the end from the starting ring securely.

HELPFUL HINTS
- This garment is very flexible, because it's not made in the usual way, it stretches and drapes to give a flattering fit.
- You can fasten your vest with just one button under the bust, as shown, or you could pin the fronts together with a brooch, use a ribbon tie or lace them together.
- If you'd like to close up the front more, simply sew on more buttons.
- Mark the buttonhole shell, maybe with a tiny loop of yarn on the wrong side, so you can find it easily.

MEASUREMENTS
To fit bust
32–34	36–38	40–42	in
81–86	91–97	102–107	cm

Actual width (across circle at widest)
34	37¾	41¾	in
86	96	106	cm

Actual length (at center back with 5½ in (14 cm) folded down for collar)
28¼	32¼	36¼	in
72	82	92	cm

In the instructions, figures are given for the smallest size first; larger sizes follow in parentheses. Where only one set of figures is given this applies to all sizes.

MATERIALS
- 10 (12:14) × 25 g balls of Rowan Lurex Shimmer in Antique White Gold 332
- C/2 (2.75 mm) crochet hook
- 1 button

GAUGE
The first 5 rounds of center back circle measure 4¼ in (11 cm), 14 rounds measure 12 in (31 cm) across using C/2 (2.75 mm) hook. Change hook size if necessary to obtain this size circle.

ABBREVIATIONS
5trcl – leaving least loop of each st on hook, work 5tr, yo and pull through all 6 loops on hook
See also page 9.

VEST

BACK
Wind yarn around finger to form a ring.
Round 1 (RS): 3 ch, 23 dc in ring, pull end to close ring, sl st in 3rd ch. [24 sts.]
Round 2: 4 ch, skip 1st st, [1 dc in next dc, 1 ch] 23 times, sl st in 3rd ch.
Round 3: 5 ch, skip 1st st, [1 dc in next dc, 2 ch] 23 times, sl st in 3rd ch.
Round 4: 6 ch, skip 1st st, [1 dc in next dc, 3 ch] 23 times, sl st in 3rd ch.
Round 5: 7 ch, skip 1st st, [1 dc in next dc, 4 ch] 23 times, sl st in 3rd ch.

Round 6: 8 ch, skip 1st st, [1 dc in next tdcr, 5 ch] 23 times, sl st in 3rd ch.

Round 7: 4 ch, leaving last loop of each st on hook, work 4 tr in first 5 ch sp, yo and pull through all 5 loops on hook, [5 ch, 1 sc in next 5 ch sp, 5 ch, 5trcl in foll 5 ch sp] 11 times, 5 ch, 1 sc in next 5 ch sp, 2 ch, 1 dc in 4th ch.

Round 8: 4 ch, leaving last loop of each st on hook, work 4 tr in sp formed by dc, yo and pull through 5 loops on hook, 5 ch, 5trcl in next 5 ch sp, [10 ch, 5trcl in next 5 ch sp, 5 ch, 5trcl in foll 5 ch sp] 11 times, 10 ch, sl st in 4th ch.

Round 9: Sl st in 1st 5 ch sp, 4 ch, leaving last loop of each st on hook, work 4 tr in first 5 ch sp, yo and pull through 5 loops on hook, * 5 ch, 1 sc in next 10 ch sp, [5 ch, 1 sc in same 10 ch sp] 3 times, 5 ch, 5trcl in next 5 ch sp, rep from * 10 more times, 5 ch, 1 sc in next 10 ch sp, [5 ch, 1 sc in same 10 ch sp] 3 times, 5 ch, sl st in 4th ch.

Round 10: 8 ch, * 1 dc in next 3 ch sp, [3 ch, 1 dc in foll 3 ch sp] twice, 5 ch, 1 dc in 5trcl, 5 ch, rep from * 10 more times, 1 dc in next 3 ch sp, [3 ch, 1 dc in foll 3 ch sp] twice, 5 ch, sl st in 3rd ch.

Round 11: Sl st in 1st sp, 5 ch, [1 tr, 1 ch] twice in same sp, * [1 tr, 1 ch] twice in each of next two 3 ch sps, [1 tr, 1 ch] 3 times in each of next two 5 ch sps, rep from * 10 times, [1 tr, 1 ch] twice in each of next two 3 ch sps, [1 tr, 1 ch] 3 times in next 5 ch sp, sl st in 4th ch.

Round 12: 1 ch, 2 sc in each 1 ch sp to end, sl st in 1st sc. [240 sts.]

Round 13: 1 ch, 1 sc in 1st sc, [5 ch, skip 3 sc, 1 sc in next sc] to end, omitting last sc, sl st in 1st sc.

Round 14: Sl st in each of 1st 3 ch, 7 ch, 1 tr, 3 ch in each 5 ch sp to end, sl st in 4th ch. Fasten off.

Round 15: This round is made up of separate flower motifs joined to the Round 14 as they are worked.

1st motif

Wind yarn around finger to form a ring.

1st motif round (RS): 4 ch, leaving last loop of each st on hook, work 4 tr in ring, yo and pull through 5 loops on hook, [5 ch, 5trcl in ring] 3 times, 2 ch, 1 dc in 1st sp after join of 14th round, 2 ch, 5trcl in ring, 2 ch, 1 dc in last sp of Round 14, 2 ch, 5trcl in ring, 5 ch, sl st in 4th ch. Fasten off.

2nd motif

Work as 1st motif but making 1st and 2nd joins in 3rd and 2nd sps from previous join, then join in the same way to adjacent 5 ch sp of previous motif after working 6th petal. Make 17 more motifs joining to edge and previous motif in the same way as 2nd motif.

20th motif

Work as 1st motif until 3 petals have been

•	sl st
○	ch
+	sc
┬	dc
‡	tr
🕸	5trcl

This charted stitch pattern shows the first
14 rounds of the vest.

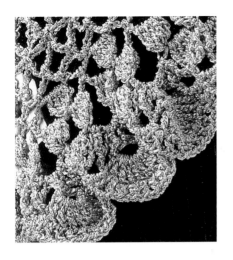

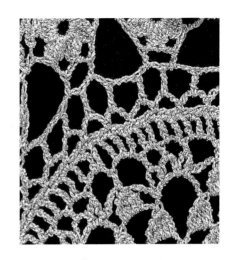

completed, join in 1st motif between 3rd and 4th petals, then join to edge and previous motif in the same way as 2nd motif.

With RS facing, join yarn in 1st 5ch sp before join between 1st and 2nd motifs.

Round 16: 5 ch, 1 dc in same sp, 2 ch, 1 tr in joined sp of 1st motif, 2 ch, * 1 dtr over join between motifs, 2 ch, 1 tr in first joined sp of next motif, 2 ch, [1 dc, 2 ch] twice in each of next two 5 ch sps, 1 tr in last joined sp of motif, 2 ch, rep from * 18 more times, 1dtr over join between motifs, 2 ch, 1 tr in first joined sp of first motif, 2 ch, [1 dc, 2 ch] twice next 5 ch sp, sl st in 3rd ch.

Round 17: 4 ch, 1 dc in first sp, 1 ch, [1 dc in next st, 1 ch, 1 dc in foll sp] to end, sl st in 3rd ch.

Round 18: 6 ch, [1 tr in next dc, 2 ch] 3 times, * leaving last loop of each st on hook, work 1 tr in each of next 5 dc, yo and pull through 6 loops on hook, 2 ch, [1 tr in next dc, 2 ch] 9 times, rep from *, 19 more times, ending last rep [1 tr in next dc, 2 ch] 5 times, sl st in 4th ch.

Round 19: 4 ch, 1 tr in 1st sp, [1 tr in next tr, 1 tr in next sp] 3 times, * skip 5trcl, [1 tr in next sp, 1 tr in next tr] 9 times, 1 tr in foll sp, rep from * 19 times, ending last rep [1 tr in next sp, 1 tr in next tr] 5 times, 1 tr in foll sp, sl st in 4th ch. [380 sts.]

Round 20: 1 ch, 1 sc in same place as sl st, 7 ch, skip 2 tr, 1 sc in next tr, 7 ch, skip

2 tr, * 1 sc in each of next 2 tr, [7 ch, skip 2 tr, 1 sc in next tr] 5 times, 7 ch, skip 2 tr, rep from * 18 times, 1 sc in each of next 2 tr, [7 ch, skip 2 tr, 1 sc in next tr] 3 times, 3 ch, skip 2 tr, 1 tr in 1st sc.

2nd and 3rd sizes

Next round: 1 ch, 1 sc in tr, [7 ch, 1 sc in next 7 ch sp] to end, 3 ch, 1 tr in 1st sc.

3rd size

Work last round again.

All sizes

120 7 ch sps.

Armhole round: 1 ch, 1 sc in tr, [4 ch, 1 sc in next 7 ch sp] 17 (19:21) times, make 64 (69:74) ch, skip next 12 (13:14) 7 ch sps for left armhole, 1 sc in next 7 ch sp, [4 ch, 1 sc in next 7 ch sp] 77 (73:69) times, make 64 (69:74) ch, skip next 12 (13:14) 7 ch sps for right armhole, sl st in 1st sc.

FRONTS AND COLLAR

Round 1: 1 ch, 1 sc in 1st sc, [7 ch, 1 sc in next sc) to left armhole, * [7 ch, 1 sc in armhole sp] 12 (13:14) times *, [7 ch, 1 sc in next sc] to right armhole, rep from * to *, 3 ch, 1 tr in 1st sc.

Round 2: 1 ch, 1 sc in tr, [7 ch, 1 sc in next 7 ch sp] to end, 3 ch, 1 tr in 1st sc.

Round 3: 1 ch, 1 sc in tr, [4 ch, 1 sc in next

7 ch sp] to end, 4 ch, sl st in 1st sc.

Round 4: 1 ch, 1 sc in 1st sc, [7 ch, 1 sc in next sc] to end, 3 ch, 1 tr in 1st sc.
Work Rounds 2, 3 and 4 two more times, then work Rounds 2 and 3 one (two:three) more times.

EDGING

Round 1: Sl st in 1st 4 ch sp, 4 ch, leaving last loop of each st on hook, work 4 tr in 1st 4 ch sp, yo and pull through 5 loops on hook, [5 ch, 1 sc in next 4 ch sp, 5 ch, 5trcl in foll 4 ch sp] 59 times, 5 ch, 1 sc in last 4 ch sp, 5 ch, sl st in 4th ch.

Round 2: Sl st in 1st 5 ch sp, 4 ch, leaving last loop of each st on hook, work 4 tr in 1st 5 ch sp, yo and pull through 5 loops on hook, [7 ch, 5trcl in next 5 ch sp, 4 ch, 5trcl in foll 5 ch sp] 59 times, 7 ch, 5trcl in last 5 ch sp, 1 tr in 4th ch.

Round 3: Sl st in tr sp, 4 ch, leaving last loop of each st on hook, work 4 tr in tr sp, yo and pull through 5 loops on hook, * [5 ch, 1 sc in next 7 ch sp] 4 times, 5 ch, 5trcl in next 4 ch sp, rep from * 58 times, [5 ch, 1 sc in last 7 ch sp] 4 times, 5 ch, sl st in 4th ch.

Round 4: 1 ch, 1 sc in same place as sl st, * 3 ch, skip next 5 ch sp, 1 dc in next 5 ch sp, 3 ch, [1 dc, 3 ch] twice in next 5 ch sp, 1 dc in next 5 ch sp, 3 ch, skip next 5 ch sp, 1 dc in 5trcl, rep from * 59 times omitting 1 dc at end of last rep, sl st in 1st sc.

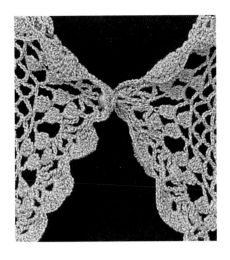
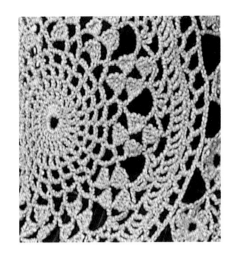
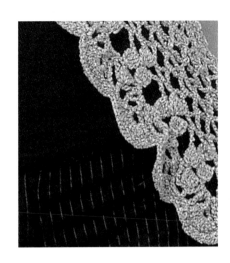

Round 5: Sl st in 1st 3 ch sp, 1 ch, [3 sc in 3 ch sp, skip next 3 ch sp, 9 tr in foll 3 ch sp, skip next 3 ch sp, 3 sc in foll 3 ch sp, 1 ch] 60 times, sl st in 1st sc.

Round 6: * 1 ch, [1 dc, 1 ch] in each of next 9 tr, 1 sc in 1 ch sp, rep from * 59 times, ending last rep sl st in 1st ch.
Fasten off.

ARMHOLE EDGINGS

With RS facing, join yarn at right under arm.

Row 1: [4 ch, 1 sc in next 7 ch sp of last round of back] 12 (13:14) times, 4 ch, sl st in dc. Do not turn.

Round 1: Sl st in 1st 4 ch sp of front, work 4 sc in each 4 ch sp around armhole, sl st in 1st sc. Fasten off.

With RS facing, join yarn at left shoulder and complete in same way as right armhole edging.

FINISHING

Weave in ends. Try on vest and decide on best place to fasten front, sew button on a shell on right front and slip button through hole in corresponding shell on left front.

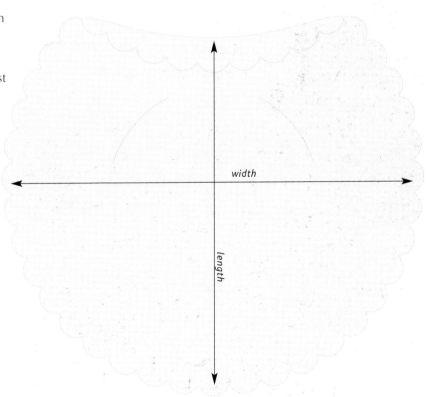

width

length

The openwork center of this lightweight wrap is worked in the Solomon's knot stitch which gives a lacy effect that is easy to work. Solomon's knot stitch is really just a series of elongated single crochet stitches. The ruffled edging is worked in double crochet.

RUFFLED MOHAIR WRAP

★☆☆ BEGINNER

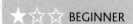 *The hook size is quite large for the thickness of the yarn. Work loosely to make it easier to insert hook when making the knots.*

To help keep the length of the loop for each knot the same, extend the stitch, then hold it between finger and thumb while working the locking stitch. If you make your stitches a different length, you may need a different amount of yarn.

There is no foundation chain for Solomon's knot stitch.

If you want to make the scarf without the frill you'll need just one ball of yarn.

HELPFUL HINTS
- Working with mohair isn't difficult as long as you keep the gauge and the stitches loose.
- If you need to unravel, ease the stitches apart, don't pull or the fibers will cling together.
- The center of the wrap will grow quickly because the stitches are so big and open.

MEASUREMENTS
Actual width (with frill)
24 in
61 cm
Actual length (with frill)
64¾ in
164.5 cm

MATERIALS
- 4 × 25 g balls of Rowan Kidsilk Haze in Candy Girl 606
- F/5 (3.75 mm) crochet hook

GAUGE
A group of four Solomon's knots measure 1¾ in (4.5 cm), 16 sts to 4 in (10 cm), 3 rows to 1½ in (3.5 cm) over double crochet using F/5 (3.75 mm) hook. Change hook size if necessary to obtain this gauge.

ABBREVIATIONS
See page 9.

WRAP

Make a slip knot on the hook and work 1 ch.
Row 1: * Draw loop on hook up to ¾ in (2 cm), yo and pull through, insert hook between loop and back strand, yo and pull through to make 2 loops on hook, yo and pull through, one knot has been completed, rep from * until 26 knots have been made.
Row 2: Skip the knot on the hook and the next 3 knots, 1 dc in center of next knot, * make 2 knots, skip 1 knot in Row 1, 1 sc in next knot, rep from * to end of row making last sc in 1 ch at beg of Row 1. There are 12 four-knot groups along short edge of wrap.
Row 3: Make 3 knots, 1 sc in next unjoined knot of previous row, * make 2 knots, 1 sc in next unjoined knot of previous row, rep from * to end.
Row 3 forms Solomon's knot stitch patt. Cont in patt until there are 35 four-knot groups along long edge of wrap. Fasten off.

EDGING
Join yarn at one corner of wrap.
Round 1: Sl st in 1st 2-knot sp, 3 ch, 14 dc in same 2-knot sp, work 15 dc in each 2-knot sp around edge of wrap, sl st in 3rd ch.
Round 2: 3 ch, 1 dc in 3rd ch, [2 dc in each dc] to end, sl st in 3rd ch.
Round 3: 3 ch, [1 dc in each dc] to end, sl st in 3rd ch. Fasten off. Weave in ends.

The size of each panel of the lacy pattern reduces to make this flattering vest flare out at the lower edge. The ribbon yarn alternates between matte cotton and shiny nylon giving a subtle change of texture as the fabric catches the light.

LONG POINTED-EDGE VEST

BEGINNER

Each point is worked separately. The points are joined and the vest is worked in one piece to the armholes, then divided for back and fronts.

The flare on the vest is made by reducing the amount of chain between double crochet group shells so the lower part of the vest is more open. After working 5 rows in double crochet shell pattern without any chain between, the width is further reduced by changing down a hook size.

HELPFUL HINTS

- It's easier to see the stitches in dark yarn if you work with a piece of light colored fabric on your lap.
- If you prefer, fasten the vest with a flower corsage, a brooch or even a tie cord made from left-over yarn

MEASUREMENTS

To fit bust

30–34	36–40	42–46	in
76–86	91–102	107–117	cm

Actual width

34	41½	49	in
86	105.5	125	cm

Actual length

29	30¾	32	in
74.5	78	81	cm

In the instructions, figures are given for the smallest size first; larger sizes follow in parentheses. Where only one set of figures is given this applies to all sizes.

MATERIALS

- 6 (8:10) × 50 g balls of Sirdar Duet in Black 745
- J/10 (6.00 mm) and I/9 (5.50 mm) crochet hooks
- 39 in (1 m) silk organza ribbon and 20 in (0.5 m) velvet ribbon (optional)

GAUGE

Each 7-row point measures 5½ in (14 cm) wide and 3 in (8 cm) high, 15 sts and 6 rows to 4 in (10 cm) measured over 1 ch dc shell patt using J/10 (6.00 mm) hook, 18 sts and 6 rows to 4 in (10 cm) over dc shell patt using I/9 (5.50 mm) hook. Change hook sizes if necessary to obtain these gauges.

ABBREVIATIONS

See page 9.

VEST

BACK AND FRONTS

1st point

Wrap yarn around finger to form a ring. Use J/10 (6.00 mm) hook.

Row 1: 3 ch, [1 dc, 1 ch, 2 dc] in ring, pull end to close ring and turn.

Row 2 (RS): Sl st in each of first 2 dc, sl st in 1 ch sp, 3 ch, 1 dc in 1 ch sp, [1 ch, 2 dc] twice in 1 ch sp.

Row 3: Sl st in each of first 2 dc, sl st in first 1 ch sp, 3 ch, [1 dc, 1 ch, 2 dc] in first 1 ch sp, 2 ch, [2 dc, 1 ch, 2 dc] in second 1 ch sp.

Row 4: Sl st in each of first 2 dc, sl st in first 1 ch sp, 3 ch, [1 dc, 1 ch, 2 dc] in first 1 ch sp, 2 ch, [2 dc, 1 ch, 2 dc] in 2 ch sp, 2 ch, [2 dc, 1 ch, 2 dc] in last 1 ch sp.

Row 5: Sl st in each of first 2 dc, sl st in first 1 ch sp, 3 ch, [1 dc, 1 ch, 2 dc] in first 1 ch sp,

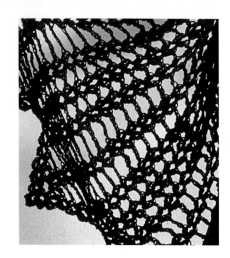

3 ch, [2 dc, 1 ch, 2 dc] in center 1 ch sp, 3 ch, [2 dc, 1 ch, 2 dc] in last 1 ch sp.

Row 6: Sl st in each of first 2 dc, sl st in first 1 ch sp, 3 ch, [1 dc, 1 ch, 2 dc] in first 1 ch sp, 4 ch, [2 dc, 1 ch, 2 dc] in center 1 ch sp, 4 ch, [2 dc, 1 ch, 2 dc] in last 1 ch sp.

Row 7: Sl st in each of first 2 dc, sl st in first 1 ch sp, 3 ch, [1 dc, 1 ch, 2 dc] in first 1 ch sp, 5 ch, [2 dc, 1 ch, 2 dc] in center 1 ch sp, 5 ch, [2 dc, 1 ch, 2 dc] in last 1 ch sp.
Fasten off.

2nd, 3rd, 4th, 5th, 6th, 7th and 8th points

Work as 1st point but before fastening off work 2 (3:4) ch, sl st in 3rd ch at beg of Row 7 of previous point.

Join edging points

With RS facing, join yarn in 1st 1 ch sp of right front point.

Row 1 (RS): 3 ch, [1 dc, 1 ch, 2 dc] in first 1 ch sp, 5 ch, [2 dc, 1 ch, 2 dc] in next 1 ch sp, 5 ch, * [2 dc, 1 ch, 2 dc] in foll 1 ch sp, [1 ch, 2 dc] 2 (4:6) times in 2 (3:4) ch sp between points, 1 ch [2 dc, 1 ch, 2 dc] in next 1 ch sp, 5 ch, [2 dc, 1 ch, 2 dc] in foll 1 ch sp, 5 ch, rep from * 6 more times, [2 dc, 1 ch, 2 dc] in last 1 ch sp.

Row 2: Sl st in each of first 2 dc, sl st in first 1 ch sp, 3 ch, [1 dc, 1 ch, 2 dc] in first 1 ch sp, * 5 ch, [2 dc, 1 ch, 2 dc] in next 1 ch sp, 5 ch, [2 dc, 1 ch, 2 dc] in foll 1 ch sp, [1 ch, skip 1 ch, 2 dc, 1 ch, 2 dc in foll 1 ch sp] 2 (3:4)

times, rep from * 6 more times, 5 ch, [2 dc, 1 ch, 2 dc] in next 1 ch sp, 5 ch, [2 dc, 1 ch, 2 dc] in last 1 ch sp. [31 (38:45) dc shells.]
Row 2 forms the 5 ch dc shell patt. Patt 4 more rows.

Next row: Sl st in each of first 2 dc, sl st in first 1 ch sp, 3 ch, [1 dc, 1 ch, 2 dc] in first 1 ch sp, * 4 ch, [2 dc, 1 ch, 2 dc] in next 1 ch sp, 4 ch, [2 dc, 1 ch, 2 dc] in foll 1 ch sp, [1 ch, skip 1 ch, 2 dc, 1 ch, 2 dc in foll 1 ch sp] 2 (3:4) times, rep from * 6 more times, 4 ch, [2 dc, 1 ch, 2 dc] in next 1 ch sp, 4 ch, [2 dc, 1 ch, 2 dc] in last 1 ch sp.
This row forms the 4 ch dc shell patt.
Patt 4 more rows.

Next row: Sl st in each of first 2 dc, sl st in first 1 ch sp, 3 ch, [1 dc, 1 ch, 2 dc] in first 1 ch sp, * 3 ch, [2 dc, 1 ch, 2 dc] in next 1 ch sp, 3 ch, [2 dc, 1 ch, 2 dc] in foll 1 ch sp, [1 ch, skip 1 ch, 2 dc, 1 ch, 2 dc in foll 1 ch sp] 2 (3:4) times, rep from * 6 more times, 3 ch, [2 dc, 1 ch, 2 dc] in next 1 ch sp, 3 ch, [2 dc, 1 ch, 2 dc] in last 1 ch sp.
This row forms 3 ch dc shell patt.
Patt 3 more rows.

Next row: Sl st in each of first 2 dc, sl st in first 1 ch sp, 3 ch, [1 dc, 1 ch, 2 dc] in first 1 ch sp, * 2 ch, [2 dc, 1 ch, 2 dc] in next 1 ch sp, 2 ch, [2 dc, 1 ch, 2 dc] in foll 1 ch sp, [1 ch, skip 1 ch, 2 dc, 1 ch, 2 dc in foll 1 ch sp] 2 (3:4) times, rep from * 6 more times, 2 ch, [2 dc, 1 ch, 2 dc] in next 1 ch sp, 2 ch,

[2 dc, 1 ch, 2 dc] in last 1 ch sp.

This row forms 2 ch dc shell patt.

Patt 2 more rows.

Next row: Sl st in each of first 2 dc, sl st in first 1 ch sp, 3 ch, [1 dc, 1 ch, 2 dc] in first 1 ch sp, * 1 ch, [2 dc, 1 ch, 2 dc] in next 1 ch sp, 1 ch, [2 dc, 1 ch, 2 dc] in foll 1 ch sp, [1 ch, skip 1 ch, 2 dc, 1 ch, 2 dc in foll 1 ch sp] 2 (3:4) times, rep from * 6 more times, 1 ch, [2 dc, 1 ch, 2 dc] in next 1 ch sp, 1 ch, [2 dc, 1 ch, 2 dc] in last 1 ch sp.

This row forms 1 ch dc shell patt.

Patt 1 more row.

Next row: Sl st in each of first 2 tr, sl st in first 1 ch sp, 3 ch, [1 dc, 1 ch, 2 dc] in first 1 ch sp, * [2 dc, 1 ch, 2 dc] in next 1 ch sp, [2 dc, 1 ch, 2 dc] in foll 1 ch sp, [skip 1 ch, 2 dc, 1 ch, 2 dc in foll 1 ch sp] 2 (3:4) times, rep from * 6 more times, [2 dc 1 ch, 2 dc] in next 1 ch sp, [2 dc, 1 ch, 2 dc] in last 1 ch sp. [31 (38:45) dc shells, 155 (190:225) sts.]

The last row forms dc shell patt. Patt 5 rows. Change to I/9 (5.50 mm) hook. Patt 2 rows.

RIGHT FRONT

Row 1 (RS): Sl st in each of first 2 dc, sl st in 1st 1 ch sp, 3 ch, 1 dc in 1st 1 ch sp, [2 dc, 1 ch, 2 dc] in each of next 5 (7:9) 1 ch sps, 2 dc in foll 1 ch sp, turn and complete right front on these sts.

Row 2: 3 ch [2 dc, 1 ch, 2 dc] in each of next 5 (7:9) 1 ch sps, 1 dc in 3rd ch.

Row 3: Skip 1st dc, sl st in each of next 2 dc, sl st in 1st 1 ch sp, 3 ch, [1 dc, 1 ch, 2 dc] in 1st 1 ch sp, [2 dc, 1 ch, 2 dc] in each of next 4 (6:8) 1 ch sps.

Row 4: Sl st in each of first 2 tr, sl st in first 1 ch sp, 3 ch, [1 dc, 1 ch, 2 dc] in 1st 1 ch sp, [2 dc, 1 ch, 2 dc] in each of next 3 (5:7) 1 ch sps, 2 dc in last 1 ch sp.

Row 5: 3 ch, [2 dc, 1 ch, 2 dc] in each of next 4 (6:8) 1 ch sps.

Row 6: Sl st in each of first 2 dc, sl st in first 1 ch sp, 3 ch, [1 dc, 1 ch, 2 dc] in first 1 ch sp, [2 dc, 1 ch, 2 dc] in each of next 3 (5:7) 1 ch sps.

Row 7: Sl st in each of first 2 dc, sl st in 1 ch sp, 3 ch, 1 dc in first 1 ch sp, [2 dc, 1 ch, 2 dc] in each of next 3 (5:7) 1 ch sps.

Row 8: Sl st in each of first 2 dc, sl st in first 1 ch sp, 3 ch, [1 dc, 1 ch, 2 dc] in first 1 ch sp, [2 dc, 1 ch, 2 dc] in each of next 2 (4:6) 1 ch sps, 1 dc in 3rd ch.

Row 9: Skip 1st dc, sl st in each of next 2 dc, sl st in first 1 ch sp, 3 ch, [1 dc, 1 ch, 2 dc] in first 1 ch sp, [2 dc, 1 ch, 2 dc] in each 1 ch sp to end. [3 (5:7) shells, 15 (25:35) sts.]

2nd and 3rd sizes only

Cont in patt, dec at front edge in same way as Rows 4 and 5 on next 2 rows. Work next row in same way as Row 6.

It's easy to keep track of how many rows of each of the chain and treble shell patterns you've worked if you place markers at each end of the last row each time you change patterns.

Each treble shell is made up of 2 tr, 1 ch, 2 tr. Remember to count each shell as 5 sts when checking your gauge.

Cont in patt, dec at front edge in same way as Rows 7 and 8 on next 2 rows. Work next row in same way as Row 9.

All sizes
[3 (4:5) shells, 15(20:25) sts.] Patt 3 (2:1) rows. Fasten off.

BACK
With RS facing, skip 1 ch sp of shell at right underarm and join yarn in next 1 ch sp.
Row 1 (RS): 3 ch, 1 dc in same 1 ch sp as joined yarn, [2 dc, 1 ch, 2 dc] in each of next 13 (16:19) 1 ch sps, 2 dc in next 1 ch sp, turn and complete back on these sts.
Row 2: 3 ch, [2 dc, 1 ch, 2 dc] in each of next 13 (16:19) 1 ch sps, 1 dc in 3rd ch.
Row 3: Skip 1st dc, sl st in each of next 2 dc, sl st in first 1 ch sp, 3 ch, [1 dc, 1 ch, 2 dc] in first 1 ch sp, [2 dc, 1 ch, 2 dc] in each 1 ch sp to end. [13 (16:19) shells, 65 (80:95) sts.] Cont in dc shell patt, work 9 (11:13) more rows. Fasten off.

LEFT FRONT
With RS facing, skip 1 ch sp of shell at left underarm and join yarn in next 1 ch sp.
Row 1 (RS): 3 ch, 1 dc in same 1 ch sp as joined yarn, [2 dc, 1 ch, 2 dc] in each of next 5 (7:9) 1 ch sps, 2 dc in last 1 ch sp.
Row 2: 3 ch, [2 dc, 1 ch, 2 dc] in each of next 5 (7:9) 1 ch sps, 1 dc in 3rd ch.

Row 3: Skip 1st dc, sl st in each of next 2 tr, sl st in 1st 1 ch sp, 3 ch, [1 dc, 1 ch, 2 dc] in 1st 1 ch sp, [2 dc, 1 ch, 2 dc] in each of next 4 (6:8) 1 ch sps.

Row 4: Sl st in each of first 2 dc, sl st in first 1 ch sp, 3 ch, 1 dc in 1st 1 ch sp, [2 dc, 1 ch, 2 dc] in each of next 4 (6:8) 1 ch sps.

Row 5: Sl st in each of first 2 tr, sl st in first 1 ch sp, 3 ch, [1 dc, 1 ch, 2 dc] in first 1 ch sp, [2 dc, 1 ch, 2 dc] in each of next 3 (5:7) 1 ch sps, 1 dc in 3rd ch.

Row 6: Skip 1st dc, sl st in each of next 2 dc, sl st in first 1 ch sp, 3 ch, [1 dc, 1 ch, 2 dc] in first 1 ch sp, [2 dc, 1 ch, 2 dc] in each of next 3 (5:7) 1 ch sps.

Row 7: Sl st in each of first 2 dc, sl st in 1st 1 ch sp, 3 ch, [1 dc, 1 ch, 2 dc] in first 1 ch sp, [2 dc, 1 ch, 2 dc] in each of next 2 (4:6) 1 ch sps, 2 dc in last 1 ch sp.

Row 8: 3 ch, [2 dc, 1 ch, 2 dc] in each of next 3 (5:7) 1 ch sps.

Row 9: Sl st in each of first 2 dc, sl st in first 1 ch sp, 3 ch, [1 dc, 1 ch, 2 dc] in first 1 ch sp, [2 dc, 1 ch, 2 dc] in each 1 ch sp to end. [3 (5:7) shells, 15 (25:35) sts.]

2nd and 3rd sizes only

Cont in patt, dec at front edge in same way as Rows 4 and 5 on next 2 rows. Work next row in same way as Row 6.

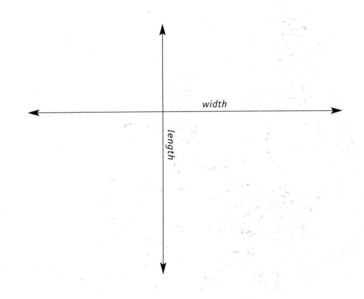

3rd size only

Cont in patt, dec at front edge in same way as Rows 7 and 8 on next 2 rows. Work next row in same way as Row 9.

All sizes

[3 (4:5) shells, 15 (20:25) sts.] Patt 3 (2:1) rows. Fasten off.

FINISHING

Matching sts, join shoulders. Leaving two long ends of the organza ribbon, make up a double bow from the two ribbons, slip ends through the last pattern before the start of the front shaping and tie.

Wrap your shoulders in this flattering, shapely shrug. It's worked in a simple double crochet with a little shell edging and the soft cotton and angora mix yarn give the garment a touch of luxury.

SHELL-EDGED SHRUG

★★☆ MEDIUM

 The shrug is worked in two sections and joined at the center back. It is designed to fit very closely.

Working a sc and 2 ch in the first double crochet instead of the usual 3 ch at the start of a row helps to close the gap after the first stitch.

Joining the sleeve and working a chain extension to use for both back and front stitches is neater than sewing the side seam.

When shaping the back and front, omitting the chain usually worked at the beginning of a row automatically decreases a stitch as there is no end chain to work into on the next row.

HELPFUL HINTS
- If you prefer, you could fasten your shrug with a brooch instead of a button.
- Always take the yarn end from the center of the ball.

MEASUREMENTS
To fit bust

32–34	36–38	in
81–86	91–97	cm

Actual width

31½	35½	in
80	90.5	cm

Actual length (including edging)

13	14	in
33	35.5	cm

Actual sleeve

20 in
51 cm

In the instructions, figures are given for the smaller size first; larger size follows in parentheses. Where only one set of figures is given this applies to both sizes.

MATERIALS
- 7 (8) × 50 g balls of Debbie Bliss Cotton Angora in Red 14
- G/6 (4.00 mm) crochet hook
- 1 button

GAUGE
13 sts to 4 in (10 cm) and 15 rows to 8 in (20 cm) measured over double crochet using G/6 (4.00 mm) hook. Change hook size if necessary to obtain this gauge.

ABBREVIATIONS
2dctog – leaving last loop of each st on hook, work 1 double crochet in each of next 2 sts, yo and pull through 3 loops on hook

3dctog – leaving last loop of each st on hook, work a double crochet in each of next 3 sts, yo and pull through 4 loops on hook
See also page 9.

SHRUG

LEFT SIDE

Make starting chain for cuff edging
Make 54 (58) ch.
Row 1 (WS): Working into top strand only, work 1 sc in 2nd ch from hook, 1 sc in each ch to end. [53 (57) sts.]
Row 2: 1 ch, sl st in 1st sc, [skip 1 sc, 4 dc in next sc, skip 1 sc, sl st in next sc] to end, do not turn, sl st in side of Row 1.

Sleeve
Row 1 (RS): Sl st in 1st starting ch, 3 ch, [1 dc in each of next 3 ch, skip 1 ch] 12 (13) times, 1 dc in each of last 4 ch. [41 (44) sts.]

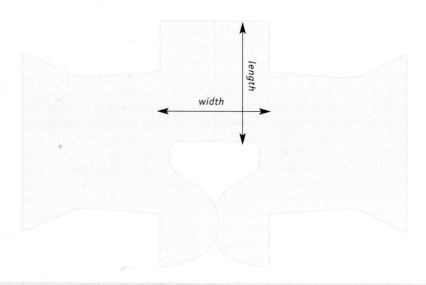

length

width

🖐 *There is no need to make a buttonhole, simply slip the button between the treble stitches at right front point.*

Row 2: 1 sc in 1st dc, 2 ch, 1 dc in each dc to last st, 1 dc in 3rd ch.

This row forms dc patt.

Working into 2nd ch at end of foll rows, cont in dc, work 6 more rows.

Dec row (RS): 1 sc in 1st dc, 2 ch, 2dctog, 1 dc in each dc to last 3 sts, 2dctog, 1 dc in 2nd ch. [39 (42) sts.]

Cont in dc, dec in this way at each end of next 4 RS rows. [31 (34) sts.]

Cont in tr, work 4 rows.

Inc row (WS): 3 ch, 1 dc in 1st dc, 1 dc in each dc to last st, 2 dc in 2nd ch. [33 (36) sts.]

Cont in dc, inc in this way at each end of 6 foll WS rows, then at each end of next 3 rows. [51 (54) sts.]

Shape for back and front

Sl st in top of 3 ch to join top of sleeve. [17 (19) ch.]

Next row (WS): Working into top loop only of ch, 1 dc in 4th ch from hook, 1 dc in each of next 13 (15) ch, 1 dc in each of 51 (54) sts of sleeve, 1 dc in each of next 15 (17) ch. [81 (88) sts.] Cont in dc, work 8 (10) rows **.

Back

Row 1 (RS): 1 sc in 1st dc, 2 ch, 1 dc in each of next 39 (43) tr, turn and complete back on these 40 (44) sts.

Dec row 1 (WS): 1 sc in 1st dc, 1 dc in each

dc to last st, 1 dc in 2nd ch.

Dec row 2: 1 sc in 1st dc, 2 ch, 1 dc in each dc to last 2 dc, 2dctog.

[38 (42) sts.] Cont in dc, work 3 more rows. Fasten off.

Front

With RS facing, skip next 19 (20) tr and join yarn in next dc.

Row 1 (RS): 3 ch, 1 dc in each dc to end. [22 (24) sts.]

Dec row 1: 1 sc in 1st dc, 1 dc in each dc to last 2 sts, 2dctog. [20 (22) sts.]

Cont in dc, dec one st in this way at each end of next 2 (3) rows. [16 sts.]

Dec row 2: 1 sc in 1st dc, 2dctog, 1 dc in each dc to last 3 sts, 3dctog. [12 sts.]

Cont in dc, dec 2 sts in this way at each end of next 2 rows. [4 sts.]

Dec one st at each end of next row. [2 sts.] Fasten off.

RIGHT SIDE

Work as given for left side to **.

Front

Row 1 (RS): 1 sc in 1st dc, 2 ch, 1 dc in each of next 21 (23) dc, turn and work on these 22 (24) sts. Complete as given for left front from Dec row 1.

Back

With RS facing, skip next 19 (20) dc and join yarn in next dc.

Row 1 (RS): 3 ch, 1 dc in each dc to end. [40 (44) sts.]

Dec row 1 (WS): 1 sc in 1st dc, 2 ch, 1 dc in each dc to last 2 sts, 2dctog.

Dec row 2: 1 sc in 1st dc, 1 dc in each dc to last st, 1 dc in 2nd ch. [38 (42) sts.] Cont in dc, work 3 more rows. With RS together, join back seam with sc.

EDGING

With RS facing, join yarn at right side seam.

Round 1 (RS): 1 ch, spacing sts evenly, work 36 (44) sc in row-ends to right front point, 18 (21) sc to neck edge, 19 (20) sc up right front neck, 26 sc across back neck, 19 (20) sc down left front neck, 18 (21) sc to left front point, 36 (44) sc to left side seam and 60 (68) sc across back, sl st in 1st sc, turn. [232 (264) sts.]

Round 2: 1 ch, 1 sc in each sc to end, sl st in 1st sc, turn.

Round 3: 1 ch, sl st in 1st sc, [skip 1 sc, 4 dc in next sc, skip 1 sc, sl st in next sc] to end, working last sl st in 1st st. Fasten off.

FINISHING

Join sleeve seams. Sew on button.

A pretty sweetheart neckline and a cut-away back make this easy-to-work tank top very special. The tank top fabric is in a simple stitch pattern with alternating rows of single crochet and filet mesh that create an open but sturdy fabric. Add paillettes for a fabulous night time look.

SPANGLED TANK TOP

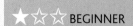 ★☆☆ BEGINNER

Always join in a new ball of yarn at the side edge, not in the middle of a row.

Do not count the 1 ch at the beginning of sc rows as a stitch.

Increases are made on filet rows but stitch counts are given after the following sc row as this is easier than remembering to count spaces on the filet row as a stitch.

When working even, the filet rows begin with a sc and 3 ch so the first hole in the mesh is the same size as the others.

HELPFUL HINTS

- The tank top is worked from the top down. This makes shaping the front neck easier and avoids the possibility of a tight lower edge.
- The pattern is very simple but because the rows are different, it's easy to know which is a right side row when shaping.
- Cathay is a cotton, viscose, and silk mix yarn with a lovely sheen and is available in twelve jewel-like shades. Sew the paillettes on afterwards so that you can match them to the yarn or add any mix of shapes and colors you like. Or you can decorate the top with beads instead.
- If you don't want to add the paillettes, you can layer the tank top over a t-shirt for a more sporty, daytime look.

MEASUREMENTS
To fit bust

32–34	36–38	40–42	in
81–86	91–97	102–107	cm

Actual width

34½	39¾	43	in
87.5	101	110	cm

Actual length

20¼	21	21½	in
51.5	53	54.5	cm

In the instructions, figures are given for the smallest size first; larger sizes follow in parentheses. Where only one set of figures is given this applies to all sizes.

MATERIALS
- 5 (6:7) × 50 g balls of Debbie Bliss Cathay in Purple 12
- F/5 (3.75 mm) crochet hook
- approximately 600 large pailette sequins (optional)

GAUGE
18 sts and 13 rows to 4 in (10 cm) measured over filet and sc patt using F/5 (3.75 mm) hook. Change hook size if necessary to obtain this gauge.

ABBREVIATIONS
See page 9.

TANK TOP

BACK
Make 36 (40:44) ch.

Row 1 (WS): 1 sc in 2nd ch from hook, 1 sc in each ch to end. [35 (39:43) sts.]

Row 2 (RS): 1 sc in 1st sc, 3 ch, skip 1 sc, 1 tr in next sc [1 ch, skip 1 sc, 1 dc in next sc] to end.

Row 3: 1 ch, 1 sc in 1st dc, [1 sc in next 1 ch sp, 1 sc in next dc] to last 2 sts, 1 sc in last

1 ch sp, 1 sc in 2nd ch.
Rows 2 and 3 form the filet and sc patt.
Patt 12 more rows, ending with a sc row.

Shape armholes

Inc row (RS): 4 ch, 1 dc in 1st sc, [1 ch, skip 1 sc, 1 dc in next sc] to end, 1 ch, 1 dc in last sc again.

Next row: 1 ch, 1 sc in 1st dc, [1 sc in next 1 ch sp, 1 sc in next dc] to last dc, 1 sc in 4 ch sp, 1 sc in 3rd ch. [39 (43:47) sts.]

Cont in patt, inc in this way on next 6 (7:8) RS rows. [63 (71:79) sts.] Do not turn at end of last row, make 9 (11:11) ch, turn.

Next row (WS): 1 dc in 2nd ch from hook, 1 dc in each of next 7 (9:9) ch, 1 dc in 1st dc, [1 sc in next 1 ch sp, 1 sc in next dc] to last dc, 1 sc in 4 ch sp, 1 sc in 3rd ch, remove hook and using spare yarn make 8 (10:10) ch, slip loop of last sc back on to hook and work 1 sc in each of next 8 (10:10) ch.
[79 (89:99) sts.]

** Cont in patt, work even for 18 rows.

Dec row 1 (RS): 1 sc in 1st dc, 2 ch, skip 1st sc, [1 dc in next sc, 1 ch, skip 1 sc] to last 3 sc, 1 dc in next sc, skip 1 sc, 1 dc in last sc.

Dec row 2: 1 ch, skip 1st sc, [1 sc in next dc, 1 sc in next 1 ch sp] to last dc, 1 sc in last dc. [75 (87:95) sts.]

Patt 4 rows even. Work 1st and 2nd dec rows again. [71 (83:91) sts.]

Patt 12 rows straight. Fasten off.

FRONT

First side

Strap: Make 4 ch.

Row 1 (WS): 1 dc in 2nd ch from hook, 1 sc in each of next 2 ch. [3 sts.]

Row 2: 1 sc in 1st sc, 3 ch, skip 2nd sc, 1 dc in 3rd sc.

Row 3: 1 ch, 1 sc in dc, 1 sc in sp, 1 sc in 2nd ch.

Rows 2 and 3 form strap patt.

Patt 12 more rows.

Shape front

Row 1: 4 ch, 1 dc in 1st sc, 1 ch, skip 2nd sc, 1 dc in 3rd sc, 1 ch, 1 dc in 3rd sc again.

Row 2: 1 ch, 1 sc in 1st dc, [1 sc in next 1 ch sp, 1 sc in next dc] twice, 1 sc in last 4 ch sp, 1 sc in 3rd ch. [7 sts.]

Row 3: 4 ch, 1 dc in 1st sc, [1 ch, skip 1 sc, 1 dc in next sc] 3 times, 1 ch, 1 dc in last sc again.

Row 4: 1 ch, 1 sc in 1st dc, [1 sc in next 1 ch sp, 1 sc in next dc] 4 times, 1 sc in last 4 ch sp, 1 sc in 3rd ch. [11 sts.]

Row 5: 4 ch, 1 dc in 1st sc, [1 ch, skip 1 sc, 1 dc in next sc] to end, 1 ch, 1 dc in last sc again.

Row 6: 1 ch, 1 sc in 1st dc, 1 sc in 1st sp, [1 sc in next dc, 1 sc in next sp] to end, 1 sc in 3rd ch. [15 sts.]

Cont in filet and sc patt, increasing as set at each end of next 4 (5:6) RS rows.
[31 (35:39) sts.] Fasten off.

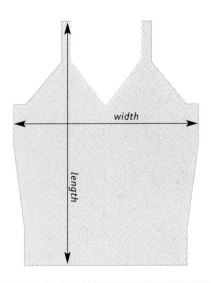

width

length

Preparation for armhole

Without turning work, join yarn at opposite end of last row and make 8 (10:10) ch. Fasten off.

Second side

Work as given for first side but do not fasten off after last row.

Preparation for armhole

Do not turn, make 9 (11:11) ch, turn.

Joining row (WS): Across second side work 1 sc in 2nd ch from hook, 1 sc in each of next 7 (9:9) ch, * 1 sc in 1st dc, 1 sc in 1st 1 ch sp, [1 sc in next dc, 1 sc in next sp] 14 (16:18) times, 1 sc in 3rd ch *, 1 ch, rep from * to * across first side, 1 sc in each of 8 (10:10) ch. [79 (91:99) sts.]

Complete as given for back from ** to end.

NECK EDGING

Matching sts, join shoulders. With RS facing, join yarn at right shoulder seam.

Round 1: 1 ch, 1 sc in each of 29 (33:37) sc across back neck, 41 (44:47) sc in row-ends to center front, 1 sc in 1 ch sp at center front, 41 (44:47) sc in row-ends to right shoulder, sl st in 1st sc, do not turn.

Round 2: Work crab st (reverse single crochet) in each st to end. Fasten off and weave in ends.

ARMHOLE EDGINGS

Join side seams. With RS facing, join yarn at side seam.

Row 1 (RS): 1 ch, 1 sc in each ch along armhole edge, 41 (44:47) sc in row-ends to shoulder, 41 (44:47) sc in row-ends to armhole edge, 1 sc in each ch to side seam, sl st in 1st sc, do not turn.

Round 2: Work crab st (reverse single crochet) in each st to end, fasten off and weave in ends.

LOWER EDGING

With RS facing, join yarn at side seam and work in crab st (reverse single crochet) around lower edge. Fasten off and weave in ends.

TO DECORATE

Using a slim, sharp needle, sew sequins on front of tank top, following the filet rows but scattering the sequins so some of the crochet fabric shows. If you secure each sequin with several small over-sew stitches there's no need to fasten off each time you sew on a sequin, simply slip the needle along the back of the crochet stitches to place the next sequin.

To space the sc evenly around neck and armhole edgings, work 1 sc in each dc row-end and 2 sc in each filet row-end.

There's no need to buy matching thread to sew on the sequins, simply cut a length of Cathay and tease out the separate strands.

The pailettes used in the picture have holes at the top so they hang down when sewn on.

FUNKY FUR CAPELET

Keep bare shoulders warm with this luxurious little wrap or wear it close to the neckline of a sweater to create the look of a glamourous fur collar.

BEGINNER

There is no right or wrong side to the fabric.

Working a sc and 2 ch into the first double crochet stitch instead of the usual 3 turning chain helps to close the gap between the first and second stitches. Loosen the loop on the hook slightly before working the sc. Work the 2nd chain a little bit loosely as this will make it easier to work into on the next row.

Placing markers on the last increase row makes it easier to measure the length of the wrap.

HELPFUL HINTS

- You can join in new yarn anywhere during a row, just work over the ends and they will be hidden in the dense pile.
- The wrap is in double crochet. The furry texture hides the stitches so when you need to count rows, hold the work up to the light.
- Use the end from the center of the ball; the furry strands will pull through more smoothly as you crochet.

MEASUREMENTS

Actual width

8 in

20 cm

Actual length (excluding ties)

38 in

96 cm

MATERIALS

- 4 × 50 g balls of Sirdar Funky Fur in Inky Blue 530
- F/5 (3.75 mm) crochet hook

GAUGE

18 sts and 11 rows to 4 in (10 cm) measured over treble using US F5 (3.75 mm) hook. Change hook size if necessary to obtain this gauge.

ABBREVIATIONS

2dctog – leaving last loop of each st on hook, work 1 dc in each of next 2 sts, yo and pull through all 3 loops on hook

4dctog – work in same way as 2dctog in each of 4 sts, yo and pull through all 5 loops on hook

See also page 9.

CAPELET

First tie

Row 1: Make one ch quite loosely, then make 3 more ch, work 3 dc in 1st ch. [4 sts.]

Row 2: 1 sc in 1st dc, 2 ch, 1 dc in 1st dc, 1 dc in each of next 2 dc, 2 dc in 3rd ch. [6 sts.]

Row 3: 1 sc in 1st dc, 2 ch, 1 dc in each dc to last st, 1 dc in 2nd ch.

Row 3 forms double crochet. Cont in dc, work 10 more rows.

Shape front

Inc row 1: 1 sc in 1st dc, 2 ch, 1 dc in 1st dc, 2 dc in each of next 4 dc, 2 dc in 2nd ch. [12 sts.]

Inc row 2: 1 sc in 1st dc, 2 ch, 1 dc in 1st dc, 2 dc in each of next 10 dc, 2 dc in 2nd ch. [24 sts.]

Cont in dc, inc one st in same way as Row 2 of tie at each end of next 6 rows. [36 sts.] Place markers at each end of last row.

Cont in dc, work even until wrap measures 32¼ in (82 cm) from markers.

Shape front

Dec row 1: 1 sc in 1st dc, 2 ch, 2dctog, 1 dc in each dc to last 3 sts, 2dctog, 1 dc in 2nd ch. [34 sts.]

Cont in dc, dec in this way at each end of next 5 rows. [24 sts.]

Dec row 2: [2dctog] 12 times. [12 sts.]

Dec row 3: [2dctog] 6 times. [6 sts.]

Second tie

Cont in dc, work 11 rows. Dec one st in same way as before at each end of next row. [4 sts.] 4dctog. Work 1 ch. Fasten off.

Simple filet mesh takes on a glamorous look in metallic yarn decorated with beads. Whatever you're wearing, add this jewelled scarf for instant party!

BEADED EVENING SCARF

HELPFUL HINTS

- Working with beads isn't difficult as long as you choose beads that slide easily along the yarn.
- Pour the beads out into a shallow dish, then it's easy to pick them up without spilling them.
- You can use a mix of different beads or you could match the color of the beads to your outfit.
- Joining new thread while making the fringe could leave a weak place, so take about 157 in (4 m) of gold thread and join the center of the thread to the center stitch of the short edge of the scarf to make two lengths and work out from the center.

MEASUREMENTS

Actual width (without beads)
2½ in
6 cm
Actual length (including tassels)
59 in
150 cm

MATERIALS

- 2 × 25 g balls of Coats Anchor Arista in gold 300
- C/2 (2.75 mm) crochet hook
- 340 medium size matte and shiny glass beads

- 440 small glass beads and 22 larger beads
- gold sewing thread
- long, slim needle

GAUGE

10 beaded filet spaces of 1 tr, 1B, plus 1 tr at end measure 3½ in (9 cm), 10 filet spaces of 1 tr, 1 ch, plus 1 tr at end measure 2½ in (6 cm), 8 rows to 4 in (10 cm) over filet patt using C/2 (2.75 mm) hook. Change hook size if necessary to obtain this gauge.

ABBREVIATIONS

1B – slide a bead up close to the work and elongating loop on hook, work 1 ch to hold bead in place
See also page 9.

SCARF

Make slipknot on hook, [1ch, 1B] 10 times, 5 ch, turn.
Row 1: [1B, 1 tr in ch between beads] 9 times, 1B, 1 tr in last ch.
Row 2: 4 ch, [1B, 1 tr in next dtr] 9 times, 1B, 1 tr in 4th ch.
Row 2 forms beaded filet patt.
Working last tr in 4th ch, work 14 more rows. 170 beads have been used. Cont with unbeaded yarn, joining in 2nd ball and sliding beads along until needed.

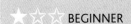

BEGINNER ★☆☆

Thread 170 of the larger beads onto the first ball of yarn and the remaining 170 onto the second ball before starting to work the scarf. To do this, thread a slim needle with a short length of sewing cotton, tie the ends in a knot to make a loop and slide the knot to one side. Pass the end of the yarn through the loop, pick up the beads with the needle a few at a time and slide them down onto the yarn.

The fringe uses smaller gold glass beads, plus a rocaille bead at the end of each strand.

You can add any beads you like to crochet as long as you make sure that they have a hole big enough to allow them to slide easily along the yarn. The original scarf mixes medium-size shiny gold glass beads and matt-coated gold beads, rocailles size 5/0.

Next row: 5 ch, [1 tr in next tr, 1 ch] 9 times, 1 tr in 4th ch.

This row forms filet patt. Work 79 more rows with unbeaded yarn, then work 17 rows of beaded filet patt. Fasten off.

FRINGE

Using a long, slim needle and leaving half of the thread free, join a 4½-yard (4-m) length of gold sewing thread to the center stitch of one short end of the scarf. Pick up 20 beads with the needle and slide them up close to the work, pick up one larger bead, then taking thread over this bead, slip needle down through the smaller beads, pull thread to tension beads so the strand is flexible but there are no gaps and secure with a few small oversew stitches. Slip needle through edge of scarf to next stitch in the filet pattern and repeat until each filet stitch is finished with a strand of small beads. Fringe the other end in the same way.

SUPPLIERS AND USEFUL ADDRESSES

USA

YARN

Accordis Acrylic Fibers
15720 John J.Delaney Dr.
Suite 204
Charlotte, NC 28277-2747
www.courtelle.com

Berroco, Inc
Elmdale Rd.
Uxbridge, MA 01569
Tel: (508) 278-2527

Boye Needle/Wrights
South St.
W.Warren, MA 01092
www.wrights.com

Brown Sheep Co., INC.
100662 Country Rd. 16
Scottsbluff, NE 69361
Tel: (308) 635-2198

Cherry Tree Hill Yarn
52 Church St.
Barton, VT 05822
Tel: (802) 525-3311

Coats & Clark
Consumer Services
P.O. Box 12229
Greeneville, SC 29612-0224
Tel: (800) 648-1479
www.coatsandclark.com

Dale of Norway, Inc.
6W23390 Stonebridge Dr.,
Waukesha, WI 53186
Tel: (262) 544-1996

Elite Yarns
300 Jackson St.
Lowell, MA 01852
Tel: (978) 453-2837

Herrschners Inc.
2800 Hoover Rd.
Stevens Point, WI 54481
www.herrschners.com

JCA Inc.
35 Scales Lane
Townsend, MA 01469
Tel: (978) 597-3002

Knitting Fever Inc.
PO Box 502
Roosevelt, NY 11575
Tel: (516) 546 3600
Fax: (516) 546 6871
www.knittingfever.com

Lion Brand Yarn Co.
34 West 15th St.
New York, NY 10011
Tel: (212) 243-8995

Personal Threads
8025 West Dodge Rd.
Omaha, NE 68114
Tel: (800) 3306-7733
www.personalthreads.com

Red Heart ® Yarns
Two Lakepointe Plaza
4135 So. Stream Blvd.
Charlotte, NC 28217
www.coatsandclark.com

Rowan USA/
  Westminister Fibers, Inc.
4 Townsend West, Unit 8
Nashua, NH 03063
Tel: (603) 886-5041
www.knitrowan.com

Solutia/Acrilan ® Fibers
320 Interstate N. Pkwy., Suite 500
Atlanta, GA 30339
www.themartyarns.com

TMA Yarns
206 W. 140th St.
Los Angeles, CA 90061

Trendsetter Yarns
16742 Stagg St.
Van Nuys, CA 91406
Tel: (818) 780-5497

Unique Kolours
23 North Bacton Hill Rd.
Malvern, PA 19355
Tel: (610) 280-7720

Yarns and …
26440 Southfield Rd.
Lower Level #3
Lathrup Village, MI 48076-4551
Tel: (800) 520-YARN
www.yarns-and.com

BEADS

Michaels
350 Walt Whitman Rd.
Huntington Station,
NY 11746-8704
Tel: (631) 423-0381
www.michaels.com

M& J Trimming
1008 Sixth Avenue
New York, NY 10018
212 391-6200
www.mjtrim.com

CANADA

Diamond Yarn of Canada Ltd.
155 Martin Ross Ave.
North York, ON M3J 2L9
Tel: (416) 736-6111
or
9697 St Laurent
Montreal, OC H3L 2N1
Tel: (514) 388-6188

S.R.Kertzer, Ltd
105A Winges Rd.
Woodbridge, ON L4L 6C2
Tel: (800) 263-2354
www.kertzer.com

Koigu Wool Designs
RR1
Chatsworth, ON NOH 3H3
Tel: (519) 794-3066

Lily ®
320 Livingston Ave. S.
Listowel, ON N4W 3H3
Tel: (519) 291-3780

Patons ®
320 Livingston Ave. S.
Listowel, ON N4W 3H3
www.patonsyarns.com

INDEX

ACKNOWLEDGEMENTS

A huge thank you to everyone who helped me with this book. First of all, David Rawson for mentioning my name, Rosemary Wilkinson for giving me the opportunity to work on this project, and Clare Sayer for her patience and enthusiasm. Thanks to Sian Irvine for the lovely photographs, as well as to the models: Emma, Jo, Kat, Natalie, and Sarah. Isobel Gillan did a wonderful job designing the book as well.

Special thanks to David Rawson and all at Sirdar Spinning; Debbie Bliss and all at Designer Yarns; Kate Buller and all at Rowan, Coats and Patons, and Mike Cole at Elle for the inspirational yarns.

Thank you to Sally Buss, Pauline Webster, and Hilary Swaby for help with creating the garments and to Betty Speller, for her encouragement and for the lovely patchwork vest. Thank you to Sue Horan, the pattern checker, who did a thorough job, as ever.

And finally, I would like to dedicate this book to my mother, Hilda Griffiths, who taught me to knit and to crochet.